Addition

Name _____

Total Problems	35
Problems Correct	_____

1. 1
  + 2

2. 4
  + 7

3. 9
  + 2

4. 4
  + 1

5. 2
  + 0

6. 3
  + 5

7. 1
  + 3

8. 4
  + 4

9. 5
  + 2

10. 3
  + 3

11. 6
  + 3

12. 2
  + 3

13. 4
  + 2

14. 6
  + 2

15. 4
  + 0

16. 7
  + 3

17. 2
  + 4

18. 2
  + 7

19. 5
  + 4

20. 3
  + 0

21. 2
  + 1

22. 8
  + 3

23. 3
  + 4

24. 2
  + 5

25. 4
  + 3

26. 2
  + 9

27. 7
  + 4

28. 3
  + 2

29. 3
  + 7

30. 8
  + 2

31. 4
  + 6

32. 4
  + 9

33. 2
  + 2

34. 4
  + 8

35. 9
  + 3

Practice = Success!

1

Addition

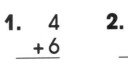

Name _____

Total Problems	35
Problems Correct	_____

1. 4
  +6

2. 7
  +3

3. 8
  +9

4. 8
  +3

5. 2
  +7

6. 9
  +6

7. 7
  +4

8. 6
  +2

9. 8
  +7

10. 3
  +5

11. 6
  +8

12. 9
  +5

13. 7
  +1

14. 8
  +4

15. 4
  +3

16. 9
  +7

17. 2
  +3

18. 9
  +8

19. 7
  +6

20. 3
  +3

21. 9
  +8

22. 5
  +8

23. 6
  +5

24. 3
  +9

25. 3
  +7

26. 8
  +8

27. 9
  +1

28. 6
  +4

29. 2
  +8

30. 3
  +2

31. 5
  +4

Practice hard. You'll win!

32. 3
  +6

33. 4
  +2

34. 9
  +4

35. 5
  +7

Addition

Name _____

Total Problems	**30**
Problems Correct	_____

1. 34
+ 52

2. 61
+ 27

3. 84
+ 14

4. 74
+ 25

5. 56
+ 33

6. 27
+ 42

7. 65
+ 21

8. 86
+ 13

9. 43
+ 25

10. 63
+ 26

11. 37
+ 45

12. 69
+ 23

13. 25
+ 79

14. 34
+ 68

15. 56
+ 37

16. 28
+ 49

17. 36
+ 25

18. 47
+ 59

19. 78
+ 16

20. 58
+ 27

21. 38
+ 97

22. 64
+ 86

Practice and anything's possible!

23. 95
+ 67

24. 85
+ 46

25. 74
+ 39

26. 68
+ 75

27. 57
+ 83

28. 64
+ 79

29. 96
+ 25

30. 89
+ 43

Math IF8740

3

Addition

Name _____

Total Problems	**25**
Problems Correct	_____

1. 23
    12
    + 54

2. 42
    26
    + 15

3. 32
    13
    + 46

4. 25
    43
    + 76

5. 78
    54
    + 21

6. 56
    43
    + 62

7. 57
    13
    + 94

8. 35
    69
    + 21

9. 27
    86
    + 33

10. 28
     64
     + 53

11. 85
     14
     + 32

12. 96
     18
     + 43

13. 45
     63
     + 32

14. 46
     58
     + 71

15. 75
     29
     + 83

16. 22
     14
     51
     + 46

17. 76
     23
     52
     + 34

18. 34
     86
     11
     + 25

19. 26
     73
     35
     + 41

20. 83
     24
     17
     + 52

21. 65
     24
     41
     + 33

22. 34
     62
     18
     + 52

Practice hard. You'll win!

23. 69
     72
     26
     + 53

24. 65
     13
     92
     + 24

25. 37
     82
     26
     + 41

4

Addition

Name _____

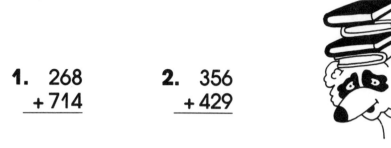

Total Problems	30
Problems Correct	_____

1. 268
    + 714

2. 356
    + 429

3. 647
    + 325

4. 208
    + 436

5. 765
    + 219

6. 524
    + 337

7. 418
    + 528

8. 368
    + 507

9. 245
    + 136

10. 478
    + 315

11. 639
    + 153

12. 257
    + 426

13. 426
    + 568

14. 349
    + 234

15. 653
    + 317

16. 396
    + 475

17. 548
    + 287

18. 297
    + 364

19. 576
    + 178

20. 259
    + 465

21. 385
    + 297

22. 463
    + 179

23. 286
    + 179

24. 167
    + 348

25. 257
    + 486

26. 394
    + 258

**Anything's possible
with practice!**

27. 679
    + 157

28. 195
    + 478

29. 584
    + 346

30. 437
    + 483

5

Addition

Name _____

| Total Problems | 30 |
| Problems Correct | _____ |

1. 268
    + 457

2. 289
    + 146

3. 378
    + 465

4. 587
    + 265

5. 459
    + 374

6. 367
    + 243

7. 586
    + 195

8. 398
    + 346

9. 286
    + 354

10. 178
     + 343

11. 567
     + 387

12. 195
     + 428

13. 689
     + 243

14. 467
     + 479

15. 268
     + 459

16. 497
     + 623

17. 486
     + 795

18. 847
     + 598

19. 369
     + 845

20. 764
     + 567

21. 565
     + 798

22. 698
     + 524

23. 478
     + 659

24. 567
     + 987

25. 878
     + 352

26. 368
     + 948

27. 869
     + 574

28. 867
     + 547

29. 764
     + 897

30. 856
     + 696

Through practice you learn!

6

Addition

Name _____

Total Problems	32
Problems Correct	_____

1. 382
    + 617

2. 735
    + 145

3. 439
    + 652

4. 579
    + 264

5. 628
    + 897

6. 905
    + 438

7. 785
    + 596

8. 365
    + 378

9. 769
    + 583

10. 486
    + 697

11. 685
    + 987

12. 897
    + 758

13. 503
    + 478

14. 728
    + 659

15. 368
    + 798

16. 749
    + 589

17. 3,268
    + 2,495

18. 6,912
    + 7,835

19. 5,782
    + 6,874

20. 3,964
    + 8,723

21. 4,852
    + 2,613

22. 8,714
    + 3,193

23. 7,135
    + 8,296

24. 3,265
    + 7,198

25. 4,382
    + 7,957

26. 6,254
    + 5,817

27. 8,152
    + 1,369

28. 8,674
    + 8,529

29. 5,136
    + 3,278

30. 8,769
    + 5,378

Practice hard. You'll win.

31. 2,103
    + 8,936

32. 8,966
    + 5,423

7

Addition

Name _____

Total Problems   24

Problems Correct _____

1. 3,610
   + 2,874

2. 8,317
   + 4,826

3. 7,246
   + 8,395

4. 6,380
   + 2,947

5. 3,542
   + 4,879

6. 8,700
   + 2,600

7. 3,619
   + 2,845

8. 4,725
   + 9,436

9. 8,124
   + 6,397

10. 6,314
    + 5,842

11. 7,348
    + 5,476

12. 3,018
    + 6,493

13. 8,912
    + 3,869

14. 3,264
    + 8,758

15. 8,416
    + 5,657

16. 8,712
    + 3,499

17. 7,836
    + 4,379

18. 2,468
    + 9,877

19. 5,738
    + 5,684

20. 3,648
    + 8,497

21. 6,834
    + 7,496

22. 2,695
    + 1,849

23. 8,364
    + 3,987

24. 9,285
    + 2,938

Through practice
you learn!

Addition

Name _____

Total Problems	26
Problems Correct	_____

1. 36
    28
    +41

2. 32
    41
    +25

3. 43
    66
    +12

4. 26
    82
    +45

5. 26
    34
    +43

6. 63
    76
    +54

7. 24
    75
    +52

8. 53
    26
    +74

9. 34
    16
    +45

10. 42
     34
     +57

11. 621
     354
     +478

12. 429
     362
     +785

13. 537
     629
     +453

14. 648
     832
     +365

15. 724
     568
     +429

16. 853
     467
     +542

17. 542
     863
     +415

18. 853
     276
     +431

19. 514
     372
     +643

20. 254
     126
     +983

21. 2,657
     1,389
     +1,161

22. 8,162
     1,113
     +2,697

23. 3,432
     3,671
     +2,989

24. 6,387
     1,212
     +5,032

25. 1,291
     2,799
     +6,143

26. 8,792
     1,733
     +4,093

Practice and anything's possible!

9

Addition

Name _____

Total Problems	25
Problems Correct	_____

1. 12
15
89
+ 64

2. 47
34
86
+ 19

3. 25
86
32
+ 27

4. 16
82
54
+ 93

5. 57
15
48
+ 26

6. 21
92
68
+ 91

7. 83
17
62
+ 95

8. 64
23
46
+ 69

9. 89
49
60
+ 24

10. 86
46
35
+ 24

11. 86
42
95
+ 26

12. 94
62
53
+ 48

13. 642
653
212
+ 324

14. 521
313
245
+ 686

15. 516
723
614
+ 932

16. 216
342
175
+ 129

17. 526
247
493
+ 312

18. 724
146
237
+ 413

19. 520
614
826
+ 439

20. 821
416
324
+ 515

21. 2,146
3,257
8,912
+ 1,674

22. 5,124
3,636
2,721
+ 1,419

23. 3,214
5,946
4,823
+ 2,152

24. 5,241
1,835
6,164
+ 5,496

25. 4,162
3,648
9,731
+ 1,229

Practice brings success!

10

Addition

Name _____

Total Problems	30
Problems Correct	_____

1. 52,618
+ 19,234

2. 83,614
+ 18,129

3. 62,146
+ 29,373

4. 43,652
+ 28,934

5. 25,426
+ 63,817

6. 68,142
+ 71,528

7. 36,417
+ 28,528

8. 19,464
+ 36,925

9. 74,265
+ 19,548

10. 84,265
+ 92,381

11. 32,694
+ 89,213

12. 76,412
+ 89,258

13. 68,417
+ 47,528

14. 56,149
+ 38,273

15. 32,485
+ 86,291

16. 56,208
+ 92,489

17. 26,915
+ 64,823

18. 88,246
+ 34,193

19. 36,142
+ 31,233

20. 92,145
+ 28,362

21. 45,216
+ 29,843

22. 64,312
+ 89,248

23. 52,643
+ 89,342

24. 46,251
+ 57,484

25. 92,615
+ 63,218

26. 73,612
+ 21,429

27. 36,924
+ 52,385

28. 58,432
+ 91,251

29. 82,465
+ 19,328

30. 36,314
+ 82,808

**Practice
makes perfect!**

Subtraction

Name _____

Total Problems	35
Problems Correct	_____

1. 3
   −0

2. 6
   −4

3. 2
   −2

4. 7
   −2

5. 4
   −4

6. 3
   −3

7. 2
   −1

8. 7
   −3

9. 3
   −1

10. 8
    −2

11. 12
    −3

12. 10
    −2

13. 13
    −4

14. 4
    −3

15. 8
    −4

16. 3
    −2

17. 11
    −3

18. 6
    −3

19. 7
    −4

20. 4
    −2

21. 9
    −4

22. 5
    −3

23. 4
    −1

24. 9
    −2

25. 6
    −2

26. 11
    −4

27. 9
    −3

28. 4
    −0

29. 5
    −2

30. 10
    −3

31. 12
    −4

Practice brings success!

32. 2
    −0

33. 10
    −4

34. 8
    −3

35. 11
    −2

Subtraction

Name _____

Total Problems	36
Problems Correct	_____

1. 6
  − 1

2. 13
  − 8

3. 7
  − 0

4. 8
  − 6

5. 8
  − 0

6. 10
  − 7

7. 13
  − 6

8. 8
  − 1

9. 16
  − 7

10. 9
  − 6

11. 10
  − 6

12. 9
  − 8

13. 7
  − 1

14. 14
  − 7

15. 6
  − 0

16. 10
  − 8

17. 9
  − 7

18. 11
  − 7

19. 6
  − 6

20. 16
  − 8

21. 15
  − 7

22. 8
  − 7

23. 11
  − 8

24. 12
  − 6

25. 11
  − 6

26. 14
  − 8

27. 8
  − 8

28. 15
  − 6

29. 12
  − 8

30. 13
  − 7

31. 7
  − 6

Practice = Success!

32. 12
  − 7

33. 15
  − 8

34. 14
  − 6

35. 17
  − 8

36. 7
  − 7

Subtraction

Name _____

Total Problems	36
Problems Correct	_____

1. 9
  − 0

2. 8
  − 8

3. 17
  −9

4. 14
  − 8

5. 9
  − 1

6. 7
  − 7

7. 16
  − 9

8. 12
  − 9

9. 15
  − 8

10. 11
  − 7

11. 12
  −7

12. 13
  −9

13. 10
  − 8

14. 9
  −9

15. 13
  −7

16. 15
  −9

17. 16
  − 8

18. 11
  −8

19. 14
  −9

20. 8
  −7

21. 10
  −9

22. 17
  −9

23. 9
  − 8

24. 15
  −7

25. 14
  −7

26. 18
  −9

27. 12
  − 8

28. 17
  −7

29. 9
  −7

30. 11
  −9

31. 13
  − 8

32. 17
  − 8

33. 16
  −9

34. 10
  −7

35. 12
  −9

36. 16
  −7

Practice brings success!

Subtraction

Name _____

Total Problems	36
Problems Correct	_____

1. 7
  − 0

2. 3
  − 2

3. 9
  − 1

4. 8
  − 3

5. 11
  − 5

6. 6
  − 1

7. 6
  − 2

8. 9
  − 6

9. 5
  − 4

10. 8
  − 5

11. 9
  − 4

12. 13
  − 6

13. 6
  − 4

14. 17
  − 8

15. 5
  − 3

16. 16
  − 7

17. 13
  − 9

18. 12
  − 7

19. 14
  − 5

20. 9
  − 2

21. 11
  − 6

22. 14
  − 9

23. 8
  − 4

24. 15
  − 8

25. 8
  − 1

26. 12
  − 8

27. 4
  − 3

28. 15
  − 6

29. 10
  − 9

30. 7
  − 2

31. 16
  − 9

32. 9
  − 7

33. 7
  − 3

34. 14
  − 8

35. 10
  − 5

36. 15
  − 7

**Through practice
you learn!**

15

Subtraction

Name _____

Total Problems	30
Problems Correct	_____

1. 76
   − 25

2. 49
   − 24

3. 87
   − 35

4. 75
   − 52

5. 69
   − 28

6. 43
   − 31

7. 36
   − 14

8. 93
   − 51

9. 89
   − 68

10. 37
   − 22

11. 68
   − 42

12. 59
   − 33

13. 75
   − 44

14. 65
   − 31

15. 86
   − 52

16. 39
   − 13

17. 95
   − 63

18. 61
   − 30

19. 28
   − 16

20. 98
   − 76

21. 88
   − 23

22. 73
   − 22

23. 85
   − 32

24. 78
   − 42

25. 56
   − 23

26. 94
   − 61

Practice!
Practice!
Practice!

27. 82
   − 31

28. 76
   − 52

29. 85
   − 74

30. 99
   − 67

Subtraction

Name _____

Total Problems	**30**
Problems Correct	_____

1. 32
− 18

2. 64
− 38

3. 86
− 57

4. 70
− 28

5. 46
− 39

6. 54
− 26

7. 97
− 68

8. 80
− 73

9. 47
− 28

10. 76
− 59

11. 31
− 24

12. 52
− 35

13. 65
− 37

14. 42
− 27

15. 50
− 36

16. 73
− 46

17. 94
− 57

18. 72
− 49

19. 36
− 18

20. 85
− 27

21. 62
− 45

22. 28
− 19

23. 90
− 37

24. 57
− 28

25. 78
− 49

26. 64
− 45

**Practice takes you
to the top!**

27. 86
− 38

28. 74
− 36

29. 91
− 74

30. 65
− 47

Subtraction

Name _____

Total Problems	30
Problems Correct	_____

1. 64
   − 29

2. 86
   − 27

3. 58
   − 29

4. 76
   − 47

5. 35
   − 18

6. 98
   − 59

7. 76
   − 68

8. 84
   − 67

9. 48
   − 39

10. 302
   − 141

11. 624
   − 251

12. 500
   − 324

13. 432
   − 341

14. 824
   − 615

15. 735
   − 382

16. 652
   − 383

17. 927
   − 463

18. 563
   − 474

19. 327
   − 149

20. 635
   − 356

21. 723
   − 248

22. 436
   − 148

23. 867
   − 279

24. 548
   − 362

25. 724
   − 537

26. 489
   − 293

27. 954
   − 567

28. 635
   − 547

29. 840
   − 382

30. 700
   − 526

**Practice and
anything's possible!**

Subtraction

Name _____

Total Problems	30
Problems Correct	_____

1. 500
    – 247

2. 903
    – 625

3. 720
    – 384

4. 600
    – 324

5. 800
    – 423

6. 405
    – 237

7. 707
    – 418

8. 900
    – 629

9. 508
    – 269

10. 700
     – 546

11. 300
     – 173

12. 603
     – 287

13. 807
     – 358

14. 200
     – 148

15. 900
     – 356

16. 606
     – 327

17. 700
     – 268

18. 500
     – 243

19. 805
     – 527

20. 960
     – 382

21. 307
     – 198

22. 400
     – 173

23. 200
     – 154

24. 705
     – 328

25. 502
     – 236

26. 800
     – 387

Practice = Success!

27. 900
     – 629

28. 603
     – 248

29. 708
     – 539

30. 500
     – 238

Subtraction

Name _____

Total Problems	__30__
Problems Correct	_____

1. 437
  − 254

2. 624
  − 343

3. 857
  − 674

4. 968
  − 794

5. 546
  − 265

6. 784
  − 592

7. 358
  − 176

8. 574
  − 292

9. 843
  − 562

10. 663
  − 271

11. 951
  − 680

12. 748
  − 354

13. 429
  − 183

14. 528
  − 264

15. 824
  − 549

16. 732
  − 465

17. 423
  − 156

18. 967
  − 388

19. 678
  − 289

20. 536
  − 458

21. 827
  − 578

22. 725
  − 468

**Practice hard.
You'll win!**

23. 824
  − 637

24. 950
  − 465

25. 536
  − 248

26. 765
  − 587

27. 921
  − 536

28. 633
  − 246

29. 521
  − 255

30. 832
  − 457

Subtraction

Name _____

Total Problems ___30___

Problems Correct _____

1. 264
  − 158

2. 314
  − 246

3. 625
  − 257

4. 436
  − 169

5. 923
  − 118

6. 700
  − 335

7. 823
  − 546

8. 947
  − 682

9. 625
  − 437

10. 541
  − 387

11. 724
  − 648

12. 846
  − 359

13. 546
  − 389

14. 800
  − 435

15. 625
  − 348

16. 543
  − 287

17. 743
  − 651

18. 8,143
  − 4,382

19. 5,614
  − 2,275

20. 8,942
  − 3,258

21. 4,275
  − 1,816

22. 7,154
  − 1,275

23. 5,264
  − 2,515

24. 3,692
  − 1,218

25. 4,682
  − 1,824

26. 6,241
  − 5,526

27. 9,294
  − 8,325

28. 6,247
  − 1,428

29. 9,215
  − 6,408

30. 7,624
  − 3,859

Practice hard.
You'll win.

Subtraction

Name _____

Total Problems	24
Problems Correct	_____

1. 6,215
− 2,437

2. 9,030
− 5,284

3. 7,253
− 4,374

4. 5,362
− 2,584

5. 8,005
− 3,127

6. 9,647
− 7,879

7. 4,153
− 1,788

8. 6,254
− 3,865

9. 7,246
− 3,587

10. 8,215
− 4,568

11. 5,271
− 3,592

12. 9,275
− 3,487

13. 6,235
− 2,586

14. 8,050
− 3,172

15. 7,346
− 5,578

16. 4,281
− 2,593

17. 3,815
− 1,937

18. 9,654
− 7,786

19. 8,615
− 3,728

20. 5,182
− 1,493

21. 6,235
− 4,367

22. 4,121
− 1,865

23. 7,310
− 2,572

24. 9,218
− 7,539

**Success ahoy!
Just practice!**

Subtraction

Name _____

Total Problems ___30___

Problems Correct _____

1. 8,143
− 2,532

2. 5,146
− 2,275

3. 6,849
− 4,723

4. 9,243
− 8,127

5. 4,265
− 2,193

6. 8,546
− 4,728

7. 3,149
− 2,027

8. 5,267
− 3,428

9. 9,245
− 5,863

10. 7,648
− 4,279

11. 6,824
− 4,372

12. 8,765
− 3,828

13. 4,926
− 2,357

14. 8,643
− 4,927

15. 6,327
− 5,138

16. 3,864
− 1,927

17. 9,647
− 6,478

18. 7,524
− 5,815

19. 6,210
− 4,128

20. 8,247
− 4,562

21. 5,262
− 3,534

22. 4,893
− 1,958

23. 3,968
− 1,279

24. 8,259
− 5,767

25. 5,694
− 3,836

26. 9,265
− 6,784

27. 7,516
− 3,427

28. 6,800
− 3,468

29. 7,000
− 2,632

30. 9,214
− 4,536

**Anything's possible
with practice!**

Subtraction

Name _____

Total Problems	30
Problems Correct	_____

1. 64,826
  – 11,614

2. 89,432
  – 17,215

3. 58,409
  – 25,326

4. 96,528
  – 34,267

5. 78,642
  – 47,235

6. 92,463
  – 71,242

7. 74,628
  – 53,254

8. 67,438
  – 34,525

9. 84,159
  – 72,437

10. 57,643
  – 46,438

11. 47,658
  – 23,826

12. 87,543
  – 66,482

13. 59,487
  – 36,396

14. 97,645
  – 76,383

15. 75,623
  – 48,512

16. 64,836
  – 43,547

17. 93,815
  – 72,907

18. 74,625
  – 58,573

19. 58,427
  – 39,243

20. 86,403
  – 64,315

21. 76,427
  – 58,245

22. 53,468
  – 37,293

23. 82,614
  – 25,307

24. 64,825
  – 42,917

25. 92,824
  – 45,572

26. 49,827
  – 23,915

27. 36,248
  – 12,159

28. 71,628
  – 45,371

29. 99,846
  – 52,938

30. 56,928
  – 37,819

**With practice,
you can do it!**

Multiplication

Name _____

Total Problems	36
Problems Correct	_____

1. 4
　×2

2. 8
　×2

3. 2
　×2

4. 2
　×7

5. 1
　×2

6. 5
　×2

7. 2
　×6

8. 8
　×2

9. 3
　×2

10. 2
　×1

11. 2
　×4

12. 2
　×6

13. 2
　×9

14. 0
　×2

15. 2
　×2

16. 7
　×2

17. 2
　×5

18. 2
　×4

19. 6
　×2

20. 3
　×2

21. 2
　×1

22. 2
　×5

23. 2
　×8

24. 9
　×2

25. 2
　×0

26. 5
　×2

27. 2
　×7

28. 9
　×2

29. 2
　×2

30. 2
　×3

31. 4
　×2

Practice and anything's possible!

32. 6
　×2

33. 2
　×3

34. 2
　×9

35. 2
　×8

36. 7
　×2

Multiplication

Name _____

Total Problems	36
Problems Correct	_____

1. 0
  ×0

2. 2
  ×5

3. 3
  ×1

4. 2
  ×1

5. 3
  ×2

6. 1
  ×0

7. 6
  ×1

8. 9
  ×2

9. 7
  ×0

10. 0
  ×2

11. 1
  ×7

12. 4
  ×2

13. 6
  ×0

14. 5
  ×2

15. 2
  ×3

16. 5
  ×0

17. 1
  ×9

18. 3
  ×0

19. 1
  ×1

20. 2
  ×8

21. 2
  ×0

22. 2
  ×6

23. 4
  ×1

24. 7
  ×2

25. 9
  ×0

26. 4
  ×2

27. 1
  ×2

28. 0
  ×1

29. 6
  ×2

30. 8
  ×0

31. 2
  ×2

Practice hard.

32. 2
  ×8

33. 5
  ×1

34. 2
  ×9

35. 4
  ×0

36. 1
  ×8

You'll win.

Multiplication

Name _____

Total Problems _____36_____

Problems Correct _____

1. 3
    ×2

2. 1
    ×3

3. 0
    ×3

4. 8
    ×3

5. 3
    ×4

6. 3
    ×6

7. 3
    ×3

8. 3
    ×9

9. 7
    ×3

10. 3
     ×2

11. 2
     ×3

12. 8
     ×3

13. 1
     ×3

14. 4
     ×3

15. 3
     ×8

16. 6
     ×3

17. 3
     ×3

18. 5
     ×3

19. 3
     ×9

20. 3
     ×7

21. 9
     ×3

22. 2
     ×3

23. 3
     ×1

24. 5
     ×3

25. 7
     ×3

26. 4
     ×3

27. 3
     ×8

28. 3
     ×6

29. 3
     ×0

30. 3
     ×5

31. 3
     ×3

32. 3
     ×5

33. 3
     ×7

34. 3
     ×4

35. 9
     ×3

36. 6
     ×3

Practice! Practice!
Practice!

Multiplication

Name _____

Total Problems	36
Problems Correct	_____

1. $\begin{array}{r} 1 \\ \times 3 \\ \hline \end{array}$ 2. $\begin{array}{r} 2 \\ \times 5 \\ \hline \end{array}$ 3. $\begin{array}{r} 0 \\ \times 2 \\ \hline \end{array}$

4. $\begin{array}{r} 2 \\ \times 4 \\ \hline \end{array}$ 5. $\begin{array}{r} 3 \\ \times 3 \\ \hline \end{array}$ 6. $\begin{array}{r} 3 \\ \times 6 \\ \hline \end{array}$ 7. $\begin{array}{r} 9 \\ \times 3 \\ \hline \end{array}$ 8. $\begin{array}{r} 6 \\ \times 2 \\ \hline \end{array}$ 9. $\begin{array}{r} 8 \\ \times 3 \\ \hline \end{array}$ 10. $\begin{array}{r} 8 \\ \times 2 \\ \hline \end{array}$

11. $\begin{array}{r} 2 \\ \times 3 \\ \hline \end{array}$ 12. $\begin{array}{r} 0 \\ \times 3 \\ \hline \end{array}$ 13. $\begin{array}{r} 1 \\ \times 2 \\ \hline \end{array}$ 14. $\begin{array}{r} 7 \\ \times 3 \\ \hline \end{array}$ 15. $\begin{array}{r} 3 \\ \times 2 \\ \hline \end{array}$ 16. $\begin{array}{r} 5 \\ \times 2 \\ \hline \end{array}$ 17. $\begin{array}{r} 2 \\ \times 2 \\ \hline \end{array}$

18. $\begin{array}{r} 7 \\ \times 2 \\ \hline \end{array}$ 19. $\begin{array}{r} 2 \\ \times 0 \\ \hline \end{array}$ 20. $\begin{array}{r} 2 \\ \times 8 \\ \hline \end{array}$ 21. $\begin{array}{r} 2 \\ \times 1 \\ \hline \end{array}$ 22. $\begin{array}{r} 3 \\ \times 9 \\ \hline \end{array}$ 23. $\begin{array}{r} 5 \\ \times 3 \\ \hline \end{array}$ 24. $\begin{array}{r} 2 \\ \times 7 \\ \hline \end{array}$

25. $\begin{array}{r} 2 \\ \times 6 \\ \hline \end{array}$ 26. $\begin{array}{r} 3 \\ \times 4 \\ \hline \end{array}$ 27. $\begin{array}{r} 3 \\ \times 0 \\ \hline \end{array}$ 28. $\begin{array}{r} 3 \\ \times 8 \\ \hline \end{array}$ 29. $\begin{array}{r} 6 \\ \times 3 \\ \hline \end{array}$ 30. $\begin{array}{r} 9 \\ \times 2 \\ \hline \end{array}$ 31. $\begin{array}{r} 3 \\ \times 3 \\ \hline \end{array}$

Practice brings success!

32. $\begin{array}{r} 3 \\ \times 7 \\ \hline \end{array}$ 33. $\begin{array}{r} 2 \\ \times 9 \\ \hline \end{array}$ 34. $\begin{array}{r} 4 \\ \times 3 \\ \hline \end{array}$ 35. $\begin{array}{r} 3 \\ \times 5 \\ \hline \end{array}$ 36. $\begin{array}{r} 4 \\ \times 2 \\ \hline \end{array}$

28

Multiplication

Name _____

Total Problems	35
Problems Correct	_____

```
1.   4      2.   0      3.   4
   × 4         × 4         × 1
```

```
4.   4    5.   7    6.   6    7.   4    8.   9    9.   5   10.   4
   × 2       × 4       × 4       × 3       × 4       × 4       × 8
```

```
11.   4   12.   1   13.   4   14.   4   15.   5   16.   4   17.   4
    × 9       × 4       × 3       × 7       × 4       × 4       × 7
```

```
18.   4   19.   8   20.   2   21.   6   22.   4   23.   4   24.   3
    × 4       × 4       × 4       × 4       × 0       × 6       × 4
```

```
25.   4   26.   4   27.   7   28.   4   29.   4   30.   8   31.   4
    × 2       × 8       × 4       × 5       × 9       × 4       × 4
```

Practice = Success!

```
32.   9   33.   2   34.   4   35.   4
    × 4       × 4       × 6       × 5
```

Multiplication

Name _____

Total Problems	38
Problems Correct	_____

1. 12
    × 3

2. 6
    × 2

3. 3
    × 5

4. 3
    × 9

5. 4
    × 4

6. 1
    × 2

7. 4
    × 12

8. 3
    × 4

9. 11
    × 2

10. 4
     × 3

11. 2
     × 3

12. 2
     × 7

13. 2
     × 4

14. 8
     × 3

15. 10
     × 4

16. 5
     × 2

17. 12
     × 4

18. 5
     × 4

19. 2
     × 2

20. 3
     × 6

21. 11
     × 3

22. 3
     × 1

23. 4
     × 9

24. 3
     × 11

25. 10
     × 2

26. 7
     × 3

27. 8
     × 4

28. 3
     × 2

29. 1
     × 4

30. 2
     × 8

31. 7
     × 4

32. 12
     × 2

33. 6
     × 4

34. 4
     × 2

35. 11
     × 4

Practice makes perfect!

36. 3
     × 3

37. 2
     × 9

38. 10
     × 3

     © 1990 Instructional Fair, Inc.

Multiplication

Name _____

Total Problems	__36__
Problems Correct	_____

1. 6
   ×5

2. 1
   ×5

3. 5
   ×4

4. 5
   ×3

5. 5
   ×8

6. 7
   ×5

7. 5
   ×5

8. 5
   ×9

9. 5
   ×4

10. 8
    ×5

11. 5
    ×5

12. 7
    ×5

13. 0
    ×5

14. 5
    ×2

15. 5
    ×8

16. 6
    ×5

17. 8
    ×5

18. 9
    ×5

19. 4
    ×5

20. 5
    ×1

21. 5
    ×6

22. 3
    ×5

23. 2
    ×5

24. 5
    ×7

25. 5
    ×5

26. 2
    ×5

27. 5
    ×9

28. 5
    ×3

29. 4
    ×5

30. 5
    ×2

31. 5
    ×6

Practice! Practice! Practice!

32. 5
    ×0

33. 5
    ×7

34. 9
    ×5

35. 5
    ×5

36. 3
    ×5

Multiplication

Name _____

Total Problems	36
Problems Correct	_____

1. 2
   × 4

2. 4
   × 4

3. 0
   × 5

4. 4
   × 6

5. 1
   × 4

6. 8
   × 5

7. 5
   × 5

8. 8
   × 4

9. 2
   × 5

10. 4
   × 5

11. 4
   × 2

12. 5
   × 2

13. 0
   × 4

14. 7
   × 5

15. 1
   × 5

16. 5
   × 4

17. 3
   × 4

18. 7
   × 4

19. 5
   × 3

20. 4
   × 2

21. 5
   × 8

22. 9
   × 4

23. 4
   × 3

24. 5
   × 5

25. 4
   × 8

26. 4
   × 1

27. 5
   × 7

28. 3
   × 5

29. 5
   × 9

30. 6
   × 4

31. 4
   × 9

Practice brings success!

32. 9
   × 5

33. 5
   × 6

34. 5
   × 3

35. 4
   × 7

36. 6
   × 5

Multiplication

Name _____

Total Problems	36
Problems Correct	_____

1.   3
  × 3

2.   5
  × 4

3.   1
  × 2

4.   3
  × 1

5.   8
  × 4

6.   2
  × 3

7.   4
  × 5

8.   5
  × 2

9.   3
  × 4

10.   9
  × 3

11.   3
  × 6

12.   4
  × 9

13.   2
  × 2

14.   7
  × 5

15.   2
  × 4

16.   5
  × 1

17.   6
  × 2

18.   8
  × 2

19.   4
  × 6

20.   1
  × 4

21.   5
  × 3

22.   9
  × 5

23.   7
  × 2

24.   5
  × 6

25.   4
  × 3

26.   2
  × 5

27.   5
  × 8

28.   3
  × 2

29.   4
  × 7

30.   5
  × 5

31.   8
  × 3

Practice makes perfect!

32.   4
  × 2

33.   3
  × 5

34.   3
  × 7

35.   4
  × 4

36.   2
  × 9

Multiplication

Name _____

Total Problems	**36**
Problems Correct	_____

1. 0
   × 6

2. 6
   × 2

3. 6
   × 7

4. 6
   × 6

5. 6
   × 5

6. 3
   × 6

7. 8
   × 6

8. 6
   × 4

9. 9
   × 6

10. 5
   × 6

11. 6
   × 9

12. 7
   × 6

13. 6
   × 8

14. 6
   × 5

15. 2
   × 6

16. 4
   × 6

17. 6
   × 6

18. 6
   × 3

19. 6
   × 9

20. 1
   × 6

21. 7
   × 6

22. 6
   × 3

23. 8
   × 6

24. 6
   × 4

25. 6
   × 0

26. 2
   × 6

27. 4
   × 6

28. 6
   × 8

29. 6
   × 2

30. 6
   × 6

31. 9
   × 6

Practice hard. You'll win.

32. 6
   × 7

33. 8
   × 6

34. 5
   × 6

35. 3
   × 6

36. 6
   × 1

Multiplication

Name _____

Total Problems	36
Problems Correct	_____

1. $\begin{array}{r} 7 \\ \times 1 \\ \hline \end{array}$ 2. $\begin{array}{r} 7 \\ \times 2 \\ \hline \end{array}$ 3. $\begin{array}{r} 3 \\ \times 7 \\ \hline \end{array}$

4. $\begin{array}{r} 9 \\ \times 7 \\ \hline \end{array}$ 5. $\begin{array}{r} 7 \\ \times 7 \\ \hline \end{array}$ 6. $\begin{array}{r} 7 \\ \times 0 \\ \hline \end{array}$ 7. $\begin{array}{r} 2 \\ \times 7 \\ \hline \end{array}$ 8. $\begin{array}{r} 7 \\ \times 9 \\ \hline \end{array}$ 9. $\begin{array}{r} 7 \\ \times 5 \\ \hline \end{array}$ 10. $\begin{array}{r} 7 \\ \times 7 \\ \hline \end{array}$

11. $\begin{array}{r} 7 \\ \times 6 \\ \hline \end{array}$ 12. $\begin{array}{r} 7 \\ \times 4 \\ \hline \end{array}$ 13. $\begin{array}{r} 8 \\ \times 7 \\ \hline \end{array}$ 14. $\begin{array}{r} 3 \\ \times 7 \\ \hline \end{array}$ 15. $\begin{array}{r} 1 \\ \times 7 \\ \hline \end{array}$ 16. $\begin{array}{r} 7 \\ \times 6 \\ \hline \end{array}$ 17. $\begin{array}{r} 4 \\ \times 7 \\ \hline \end{array}$

18. $\begin{array}{r} 5 \\ \times 7 \\ \hline \end{array}$ 19. $\begin{array}{r} 9 \\ \times 7 \\ \hline \end{array}$ 20. $\begin{array}{r} 7 \\ \times 2 \\ \hline \end{array}$ 21. $\begin{array}{r} 6 \\ \times 7 \\ \hline \end{array}$ 22. $\begin{array}{r} 7 \\ \times 5 \\ \hline \end{array}$ 23. $\begin{array}{r} 7 \\ \times 7 \\ \hline \end{array}$ 24. $\begin{array}{r} 4 \\ \times 7 \\ \hline \end{array}$

25. $\begin{array}{r} 7 \\ \times 9 \\ \hline \end{array}$ 26. $\begin{array}{r} 6 \\ \times 7 \\ \hline \end{array}$ 27. $\begin{array}{r} 8 \\ \times 7 \\ \hline \end{array}$ 28. $\begin{array}{r} 7 \\ \times 3 \\ \hline \end{array}$ 29. $\begin{array}{r} 7 \\ \times 8 \\ \hline \end{array}$ 30. $\begin{array}{r} 5 \\ \times 7 \\ \hline \end{array}$ 31. $\begin{array}{r} 2 \\ \times 7 \\ \hline \end{array}$

Practice! Practice! Practice!

32. $\begin{array}{r} 7 \\ \times 4 \\ \hline \end{array}$ 33. $\begin{array}{r} 7 \\ \times 2 \\ \hline \end{array}$ 34. $\begin{array}{r} 0 \\ \times 7 \\ \hline \end{array}$ 35. $\begin{array}{r} 7 \\ \times 7 \\ \hline \end{array}$ 36. $\begin{array}{r} 7 \\ \times 8 \\ \hline \end{array}$

Multiplication

Name _____

1. 7
   × 3

2. 6
   × 2

3. 1
   × 7

4. 6
   × 5

5. 8
   × 7

6. 0
   × 6

7. 6
   × 6

8. 5
   × 7

9. 8
   × 6

10. 6
    × 7

11. 2
    × 6

12. 7
    × 4

13. 2
    × 7

14. 9
    × 6

15. 7
    × 6

16. 4
    × 6

17. 7
    × 7

18. 0
    × 7

19. 5
    × 6

20. 9
    × 7

21. 6
    × 3

22. 7
    × 9

23. 6
    × 7

24. 7
    × 2

25. 7
    × 6

26. 6
    × 4

27. 7
    × 8

28. 1
    × 6

29. 4
    × 7

30. 6
    × 6

31. 7
    × 5

Practice takes you to the top!

32. 6
    × 8

33. 3
    × 7

34. 7
    × 7

35. 6
    × 9

36. 3
    × 6

Multiplication

Name _____

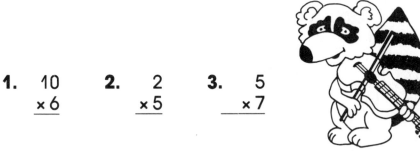

Total Problems	38
Problems Correct	_____

1.　10
　　 × 6

2.　　2
　　 × 5

3.　　5
　　 × 7

4.　　7
　　 × 5

5.　　2
　　 × 6

6.　　7
　　 × 7

7.　　6
　　 × 5

8.　 11
　　 × 7

9.　　6
　　 × 1

10.　12
　　 × 5

11.　　6
　　 × 6

12.　　8
　　 × 7

13.　　1
　　 × 5

14.　　9
　　 × 6

15.　　2
　　 × 7

16.　　5
　　 × 5

17.　 11
　　 × 6

18.　　3
　　 × 6

19.　　4
　　 × 7

20.　　7
　　 × 12

21.　 10
　　 × 5

22.　　6
　　 × 7

23.　 10
　　 × 7

24.　 11
　　 × 5

25.　　1
　　 × 7

26.　　3
　　 × 5

27.　　7
　　 × 9

28.　　4
　　 × 6

29.　　6
　　 × 12

30.　　4
　　 × 5

31.　　7
　　 × 6

32.　 12
　　 × 6

33.　　8
　　 × 5

34.　 12
　　 × 7

35.　　5
　　 × 6

Practice brings success!

36.　　3
　　 × 7

37.　　9
　　 × 5

38.　　8
　　 × 6

Multiplication

Name _____

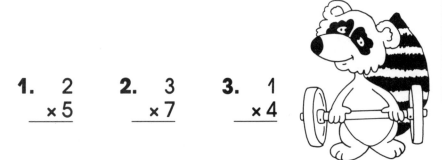

Total Problems	__36__
Problems Correct	_____

1. 2
   × 5

2. 3
   × 7

3. 1
   × 4

4. 4
   × 6

5. 3
   × 4

6. 5
   × 5

7. 1
   × 6

8. 7
   × 4

9. 4
   × 5

10. 9
    × 6

11. 5
    × 1

12. 6
    × 5

13. 4
    × 2

14. 7
    × 1

15. 7
    × 5

16. 9
    × 7

17. 6
    × 4

18. 6
    × 3

19. 4
    × 8

20. 7
    × 6

21. 5
    × 3

22. 4
    × 7

23. 4
    × 9

24. 7
    × 7

25. 5
    × 6

26. 6
    × 7

27. 8
    × 6

28. 4
    × 4

29. 2
    × 6

30. 2
    × 7

31. 9
    × 5

With practice, you can do it!

32. 5
    × 7

33. 5
    × 4

34. 8
    × 7

35. 6
    × 6

36. 8
    × 5

Multiplication

Name _____

Total Problems	36
Problems Correct	_____

1. 1
×8

2. 8
×5

3. 8
×3

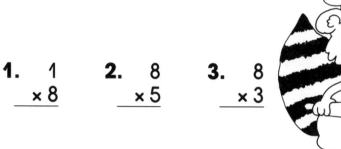

4. 8
×9

5. 0
×8

6. 7
×8

7. 8
×4

8. 6
×8

9. 8
×2

10. 5
×8

11. 8
×8

12. 5
×8

13. 9
×8

14. 8
×7

15. 8
×2

16. 4
×8

17. 6
×8

18. 3
×8

19. 8
×6

20. 2
×8

21. 8
×8

22. 8
×6

23. 2
×8

24. 9
×8

25. 8
×4

26. 8
×8

27. 7
×8

28. 8
×1

29. 4
×8

30. 8
×8

31. 8
×3

Anything's possible with practice!

32. 8
×0

33. 8
×9

34. 8
×7

35. 3
×8

36. 8
×5

Multiplication

Name _____

Total Problems	36
Problems Correct	_____

1. 1
   ×9

2. 4
   ×9

3. 9
   ×2

4. 9
   ×5

5. 0
   ×9

6. 3
   ×9

7. 9
   ×7

8. 6
   ×9

9. 7
   ×9

10. 9
    ×4

11. 7
    ×9

12. 9
    ×1

13. 9
    ×9

14. 9
    ×3

15. 9
    ×5

16. 8
    ×9

17. 5
    ×9

18. 9
    ×6

19. 9
    ×9

20. 2
    ×9

21. 9
    ×0

22. 9
    ×8

23. 4
    ×9

24. 9
    ×6

25. 9
    ×8

26. 9
    ×3

27. 5
    ×9

28. 9
    ×9

29. 9
    ×7

30. 9
    ×2

31. 8
    ×9

Practice hard. You'll win.

32. 9
    ×9

33. 2
    ×9

34. 9
    ×4

35. 6
    ×9

36. 3
    ×9

Multiplication

Name _____

Total Problems	36
Problems Correct	_____

1.　5
　×9

2.　2
　×8

3.　0
　×9

4.　9
　×8

5.　0
　×8

6.　9
　×4

7.　8
　×5

8.　9
　×2

9.　9
　×8

10.　9
　×9

11.　8
　×8

12.　2
　×9

13.　8
　×6

14.　9
　×5

15.　3
　×8

16.　1
　×9

17.　8
　×8

18.　4
　×8

19.　8
　×7

20.　6
　×9

21.　8
　×2

22.　8
　×9

23.　5
　×8

24.　9
　×6

25.　7
　×9

26.　8
　×3

27.　1
　×8

28.　3
　×9

29.　9
　×9

30.　7
　×8

31.　9
　×3

Practice and anything's possible!

32.　8
　×9

33.　9
　×7

34.　4
　×9

35.　6
　×8

36.　8
　×4

Multiplication

Name _____

Total Problems	36
Problems Correct	_____

1. 8
   ×2

2. 4
   ×6

3. 7
   ×1

4. 9
   ×6

5. 8
   ×8

6. 7
   ×5

7. 1
   ×6

8. 8
   ×7

9. 8
   ×6

10. 7
   ×9

11. 7
   ×4

12. 1
   ×8

13. 7
   ×8

14. 6
   ×2

15. 8
   ×5

16. 9
   ×1

17. 7
   ×6

18. 3
   ×6

19. 6
   ×8

20. 2
   ×7

21. 6
   ×9

22. 7
   ×7

23. 8
   ×9

24. 9
   ×3

25. 6
   ×7

26. 9
   ×9

27. 3
   ×8

28. 5
   ×9

29. 5
   ×6

30. 2
   ×9

31. 9
   ×8

Practice makes perfect!

32. 9
   ×7

33. 4
   ×9

34. 6
   ×6

35. 4
   ×8

36. 3
   ×7

Multiplication

Name _____

Total Problems	36
Problems Correct	_____

1. 3
  × 1

2. 2
  × 5

3. 2
  × 2

4. 6
  × 2

5. 1
  × 5

6. 4
  × 3

7. 5
  × 6

8. 5
  × 2

9. 4
  × 4

10. 2
  × 3

11. 3
  × 7

12. 5
  × 4

13. 1
  × 2

14. 3
  × 8

15. 5
  × 5

16. 4
  × 2

17. 3
  × 5

18. 7
  × 2

19. 9
  × 4

20. 3
  × 3

21. 9
  × 5

22. 2
  × 4

23. 8
  × 2

24. 7
  × 5

25. 5
  × 3

26. 1
  × 4

27. 6
  × 4

28. 3
  × 2

29. 4
  × 8

30. 4
  × 5

31. 9
  × 3

Practice brings success!

32. 6
  × 3

33. 8
  × 5

34. 7
  × 4

35. 9
  × 2

36. 3
  × 4

Multiplication

Name _____

Total Problems	36
Problems Correct	_____

1. 0
   × 7

2. 4
   × 3

3. 1
   × 5

4. 4
   × 8

5. 3
   × 6

6. 5
   × 5

7. 9
   × 6

8. 4
   × 2

9. 2
   × 6

10. 4
   × 7

11. 2
   × 5

12. 6
   × 6

13. 1
   × 4

14. 4
   × 5

15. 8
   × 6

16. 4
   × 9

17. 5
   × 6

18. 6
   × 5

19. 7
   × 3

20. 4
   × 4

21. 4
   × 6

22. 7
   × 9

23. 7
   × 5

24. 7
   × 7

25. 7
   × 4

26. 5
   × 9

27. 0
   × 6

28. 3
   × 5

29. 5
   × 7

30. 6
   × 4

31. 6
   × 7

32. 8
   × 5

33. 2
   × 7

34. 8
   × 7

35. 5
   × 4

36. 7
   × 6

Practice and anything's possible!

Multiplication

Name _____

Total Problems	36
Problems Correct	_____

1. 0
   ×8

2. 2
   ×5

3. 1
   ×6

4. 5
   ×6

5. 3
   ×8

6. 9
   ×6

7. 5
   ×7

8. 6
   ×5

9. 5
   ×8

10. 7
    ×6

11. 7
    ×5

12. 2
    ×8

13. 1
    ×7

14. 5
    ×0

15. 4
    ×7

16. 5
    ×9

17. 4
    ×8

18. 3
    ×7

19. 3
    ×5

20. 9
    ×7

21. 2
    ×6

22. 7
    ×8

23. 8
    ×5

24. 7
    ×7

25. 6
    ×6

26. 8
    ×8

27. 6
    ×7

28. 4
    ×5

29. 6
    ×8

30. 2
    ×7

31. 4
    ×6

Practice hard. You'll win.

32. 8
    ×6

33. 9
    ×8

34. 5
    ×5

35. 8
    ×7

36. 3
    ×6

Multiplication

Name _____

Total Problems	36
Problems Correct	_____

1. 3
   ×6

2. 8
   ×2

3. 4
   ×9

4. 7
   ×7

5. 5
   ×5

6. 4
   ×3

7. 6
   ×8

8. 7
   ×4

9. 7
   ×9

10. 6
    ×6

11. 5
    ×9

12. 9
    ×8

13. 5
    ×6

14. 4
    ×2

15. 6
    ×3

16. 5
    ×7

17. 9
    ×4

18. 4
    ×5

19. 7
    ×2

20. 6
    ×5

21. 8
    ×6

22. 7
    ×8

23. 9
    ×2

24. 8
    ×3

25. 8
    ×8

26. 6
    ×7

27. 6
    ×9

28. 4
    ×4

29. 5
    ×3

30. 3
    ×7

31. 8
    ×4

Practice! Practice! Practice!

32. 8
    ×5

33. 9
    ×7

34. 7
    ×3

35. 4
    ×6

36. 8
    ×9

Multiplication

Name _____

Total Problems	38
Problems Correct	_____

1. 11
    × 9

2. 8
    × 8

3. 9
    × 6

4. 3
    × 10

5. 9
    × 12

6. 8
    × 2

7. 11
    × 10

8. 12
    × 8

9. 5
    × 9

10. 9
     × 8

11. 4
     × 8

12. 7
     × 9

13. 2
     × 10

14. 1
     × 8

15. 4
     × 10

16. 11
     × 8

17. 9
     × 9

18. 9
     × 1

19. 7
     × 10

20. 8
     × 12

21. 3
     × 8

22. 10
     × 9

23. 10
     × 10

24. 8
     × 9

25. 7
     × 8

26. 1
     × 10

27. 2
     × 9

28. 9
     × 10

29. 4
     × 9

30. 6
     × 8

31. 6
     × 10

32. 12
     × 10

33. 10
     × 8

34. 5
     × 10

35. 8
     × 5

Practice! Practice! Practice!

36. 12
     × 9

37. 8
     × 10

38. 3
     × 9

Multiplication

Name _____

Total Problems	38
Problems Correct	_____

1. 11
  × 6

2.   1
  × 11

3.   5
  × 12

4.   7
  × 11

5. 12
  × 11

6. 12
  × 12

7.   4
  × 12

8.   6
  × 11

9. 11
  × 12

10. 11
  × 11

11.   5
  × 11

12. 11
  × 7

13.   6
  × 12

14. 12
  × 9

15. 10
  × 11

16. 10
  × 12

17. 12
  × 8

18.   3
  × 12

19. 11
  × 9

20.   2
  × 11

21.   9
  × 12

22. 12
  × 7

23. 11
  × 4

24.   2
  × 12

25. 12
  × 12

26.   1
  × 12

27. 11
  × 10

28.   9
  × 11

29. 12
  × 11

30.   8
  × 12

31. 11
  × 9

32. 11
  × 8

33. 12
  × 10

34.   3
  × 11

35.   7
  × 12

Practice = Success!

36. 12
  × 6

37.   8
  × 11

38. 12
  × 1

Multiplication

Name _____

Total Problems	30
Problems Correct	_____

1. 32
× 3

2. 21
× 4

3. 43
× 2

4. 20
× 3

5. 11
× 4

6. 34
× 2

7. 21
× 3

8. 33
× 3

9. 24
× 2

10. 22
× 4

11. 40
× 2

12. 32
× 2

13. 13
× 3

14. 22
× 2

15. 20
× 4

16. 23
× 2

17. 11
× 3

18. 41
× 2

19. 31
× 3

20. 44
× 2

21. 23
× 3

22. 12
× 4

23. 33
× 2

24. 30
× 3

25. 21
× 2

26. 13
× 2

Practice makes perfect!

27. 42
× 2

28. 12
× 3

29. 14
× 2

30. 22
× 3

Multiplication

Name _____

Total Problems	30
Problems Correct	_____

1. 26
    × 3

2. 24
    × 4

3. 39
    × 2

4. 14
    × 7

5. 25
    × 3

6. 13
    × 5

7. 37
    × 2

8. 48
    × 2

9. 23
    × 4

10. 35
     × 2

11. 12
     × 8

12. 24
     × 3

13. 13
     × 6

14. 18
     × 5

15. 29
     × 3

16. 17
     × 5

17. 49
     × 2

18. 16
     × 6

19. 36
     × 2

20. 18
     × 3

21. 15
     × 6

22. 27
     × 3

23. 13
     × 7

24. 28
     × 3

25. 19
     × 5

26. 46
     × 2

27. 16
     × 5

28. 47
     × 2

29. 14
     × 6

30. 53
     × 4

With practice, you can do it!

Multiplication

Name _____

Total Problems	30
Problems Correct	_____

1. 37
× 4

2. 48
× 3

3. 76
× 2

4. 59
× 4

5. 34
× 6

6. 38
× 5

7. 48
× 2

8. 45
× 6

9. 67
× 3

10. 43
× 4

11. 85
× 2

12. 39
× 5

13. 64
× 3

14. 83
× 6

15. 45
× 3

16. 63
× 5

17. 93
× 4

18. 86
× 2

19. 73
× 5

20. 66
× 4

21. 25
× 6

22. 74
× 3

23. 23
× 6

24. 97
× 2

25. 47
× 5

26. 77
× 4

**Practice takes
you to the top!**

27. 75
× 2

28. 46
× 5

29. 68
× 2

30. 84
× 4

Multiplication

Name _____

Total Problems	28
Problems Correct	_____

1. 13
× 5

2. 38
× 2

3. 14
× 8

4. 15
× 6

5. 36
× 3

6. 39
× 2

7. 27
× 4

8. 28
× 3

9. 47
× 2

10. 16
× 9

11. 15
× 5

12. 13
× 7

13. 17
× 6

14. 25
× 4

15. 24
× 3

16. 45
× 2

17. 16
× 8

18. 14
× 7

19. 29
× 2

20. 16
× 4

21. 37
× 3

22. 16
× 5

23. 48
× 2

24. 19
× 4

25. 29
× 3

Practice hard. You'll win!

26. 13
× 8

27. 18
× 6

28. 28
× 4

52

Multiplication

Name _____

| Total Problems | 30 |
| Problems Correct | _____ |

1. 26
    × 3

2. 64
    × 5

3. 43
    × 8

4. 57
    × 6

5. 98
    × 2

6. 35
    × 4

7. 76
    × 3

8. 46
    × 7

9. 85
    × 3

10. 35
    × 8

11. 23
    × 9

12. 62
    × 5

13. 42
    × 6

14. 73
    × 4

15. 82
    × 5

16. 67
    × 3

17. 27
    × 8

18. 49
    × 7

19. 88
    × 2

20. 36
    × 9

21. 53
    × 6

22. 83
    × 4

23. 65
    × 5

24. 34
    × 8

25. 47
    × 6

26. 28
    × 3

27. 34
    × 7

Practice brings success!

28. 83
    × 4

29. 35
    × 6

30. 73
    × 8

Multiplication

Name _____

Total Problems	30
Problems Correct	_____

1. 84
× 5

2. 35
× 7

3. 63
× 8

4. 57
× 4

5. 55
× 9

6. 43
× 6

7. 92
× 8

8. 42
× 9

9. 85
× 6

10. 53
× 4

11. 74
× 8

12. 83
× 5

13. 65
× 7

14. 87
× 3

15. 49
× 6

16. 23
× 9

17. 86
× 4

18. 35
× 8

19. 82
× 5

20. 32
× 9

21. 46
× 6

22. 89
× 2

**With practice,
you can do it!**

23. 64
× 7

24. 43
× 9

25. 28
× 6

26. 59
× 8

27. 72
× 5

28. 44
× 9

29. 84
× 7

30. 53
× 6

Multiplication

Name _____

Total Problems	30
Problems Correct	_____

1. 76
× 4

2. 23
× 6

3. 49
× 8

4. 64
× 5

5. 87
× 9

6. 43
× 7

7. 88
× 3

8. 73
× 6

9. 54
× 8

10. 69
× 5

11. 74
× 9

12. 39
× 7

13. 83
× 9

14. 45
× 6

15. 75
× 8

16. 62
× 7

17. 28
× 9

18. 52
× 8

19. 63
× 5

20. 77
× 3

21. 38
× 9

22. 97
× 2

23. 48
× 7

24. 53
× 9

25. 29
× 7

26. 37
× 8

**Practice puts
you on top!**

27. 57
× 6

28. 48
× 8

29. 73
× 9

30. 82
× 7

Multiplication

Name _____

Total Problems	30
Problems Correct	_____

1. 416
    × 4

2. 318
    × 6

3. 379
    × 2

4. 719
    × 9

5. 168
    × 7

6. 713
    × 8

7. 219
    × 6

8. 237
    × 5

9. 279
    × 3

10. 173
    × 9

11. 164
    × 6

12. 179
    × 8

13. 716
    × 7

14. 298
    × 4

15. 836
    × 3

16. 632
    × 5

17. 218
    × 9

18. 816
    × 8

19. 421
    × 6

20. 248
    × 2

21. 541
    × 7

22. 918
    × 4

23. 641
    × 9

24. 836
    × 3

25. 941
    × 8

26. 917
    × 6

**Practice
puts you on top!**

27. 328
    × 7

28. 812
    × 9

29. 621
    × 7

30. 713
    × 8

Multiplication

Name _____

Total Problems	30
Problems Correct	_____

1. 423
   × 6

2. 735
   × 3

3. 817
   × 9

4. 325
   × 5

5. 316
   × 8

6. 326
   × 6

7. 623
   × 4

8. 231
   × 7

9. 687
   × 3

10. 823
    × 4

11. 912
    × 9

12. 813
    × 6

13. 912
    × 8

14. 867
    × 2

15. 613
    × 7

16. 524
    × 5

17. 716
    × 6

18. 532
    × 5

19. 921
    × 8

20. 703
    × 4

21. 608
    × 9

22. 517
    × 7

Practice makes perfect!

23. 123
    × 9

24. 312
    × 7

25. 768
    × 2

26. 152
    × 6

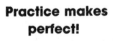

27. 353
    × 4

28. 364
    × 8

29. 524
    × 6

30. 321
    × 9

Multiplication

Name _____

Total Problems	30
Problems Correct	_____

1. 2,684
× 3

2. 9,436
× 7

3. 8,146
× 5

4. 8,938
× 2

5. 5,437
× 6

6. 8,346
× 4

7. 9,136
× 3

8. 8,324
× 9

9. 5,324
× 3

10. 2,645
× 7

11. 9,845
× 2

12. 3,247
× 6

13. 6,205
× 8

14. 3,879
× 4

15. 4,275
× 6

16. 6,248
× 3

17. 4,189
× 5

18. 7,648
× 2

19. 8,154
× 7

20. 3,264
× 8

21. 5,265
× 4

22. 4,262
× 3

23. 6,485
× 5

24. 9,134
× 8

25. 6,843
× 4

26. 9,247
× 2

27. 3,648
× 7

28. 6,527
× 2

29. 3,124
× 9

30. 6,945
× 3

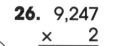

Practice hard. You'll win!

© 1990 Instructional Fair, Inc.

Multiplication

Name _____

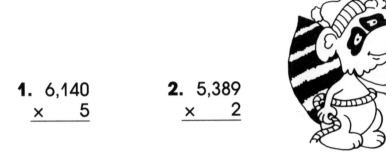

Total Problems	30
Problems Correct	_____

1. 6,140
× 5

2. 5,389
× 2

3. 6,528
× 8

4. 9,476
× 3

5. 4,326
× 7

6. 7,342
× 4

7. 9,465
× 6

8. 3,186
× 9

9. 8,547
× 5

10. 2,894
× 3

11. 2,315
× 8

12. 9,478
× 2

13. 3,272
× 6

14. 8,675
× 4

15. 4,639
× 8

16. 9,576
× 3

17. 8,964
× 5

18. 9,210
× 7

19. 3,948
× 6

20. 8,674
× 2

21. 5,782
× 4

22. 3,546
× 9

23. 3,765
× 8

24. 4,268
× 3

25. 7,286
× 5

26. 8,547
× 6

27. 8,795
× 4

28. 6,249
× 5

29. 3,742
× 9

30. 6,924
× 7

Practice puts you on top!

Multiplication

Name _____

Show your work on another sheet.
Write your answers here.

Total Problems	30
Problems Correct	_____

1. 45
   × 23

2. 53
   × 17

3. 25
   × 47

4. 48
   × 34

5. 54
   × 23

6. 32
   × 51

7. 35
   × 63

8. 44
   × 29

9. 58
   × 37

10. 39
    × 14

11. 62
    × 46

12. 36
    × 52

13. 57
    × 32

14. 49
    × 27

15. 24
    × 68

16. 37
    × 43

17. 71
    × 54

18. 35
    × 42

19. 56
    × 23

20. 39
    × 32

21. 23
    × 64

22. 43
    × 35

23. 37
    × 19

24. 42
    × 37

25. 35
    × 46

26. 53
    × 26

27. 31
    × 68

28. 36
    × 48

29. 59
    × 27

30. 28
    × 56

Practice! Practice! Practice!

Multiplication

Name _____

Show your work on another sheet.
Write your answers here.

Total Problems	30
Problems Correct	_____

1. 45
   × 38

2. 28
   × 57

3. 47
   × 63

4. 36
   × 82

5. 53
   × 74

6. 63
   × 28

7. 39
   × 45

8. 84
   × 53

9. 28
   × 39

10. 65
   × 83

11. 48
   × 63

12. 67
   × 25

13. 27
   × 49

14. 82
   × 36

15. 24
   × 93

16. 48
   × 30

17. 83
   × 62

18. 46
   × 81

19. 57
   × 38

20. 62
   × 54

21. 76
   × 46

22. 49
   × 73

23. 54
   × 18

24. 74
   × 36

25. 68
   × 24

26. 39
   × 56

27. 63
   × 42

**Anything's possible
with practice!**

28. 32
   × 84

29. 65
   × 45

30. 27
   × 34

Multiplication

Name _____

Show your work on another sheet.
Write your answers here.

Total Problems	30
Problems Correct	_____

1. 326
× 14

2. 345
× 23

3. 265
× 13

4. 416
× 25

5. 364
× 18

6. 516
× 32

7. 365
× 41

8. 423
× 51

9. 363
× 23

10. 245
× 34

11. 523
× 15

12. 142
× 28

13. 212
× 45

14. 234
× 36

15. 325
× 24

16. 232
× 19

17. 425
× 43

18. 443
× 24

19. 312
× 52

20. 286
× 34

21. 132
× 41

22. 284
× 26

23. 429
× 58

24. 235
× 28

25. 516
× 48

26. 425
× 38

27. 235
× 72

28. 142
× 63

29. 323
× 45

30. 261
× 34

Practice makes perfect!

Multiplication

Name _____

Show your work on another sheet.
Write your answers here.

Total Problems	30
Problems Correct	_____

1. 407
× 39

2. 530
× 62

3. 261
× 40

4. 704
× 82

5. 607
× 53

6. 437
× 20

7. 623
× 30

8. 140
× 57

9. 210
× 78

10. 527
× 30

11. 708
× 23

12. 283
× 40

13. 340
× 68

14. 630
× 24

15. 208
× 40

16. 896
× 30

17. 730
× 52

18. 347
× 80

19. 310
× 64

20. 488
× 20

21. 107
× 46

22. 830
× 71

23. 748
× 50

24. 560
× 36

25. 205
× 94

26. 827
× 70

27. 736
× 20

28. 506
× 44

29. 830
× 64

30. 463
× 50

**Practice hard.
You'll win.**

Multiplication

Name _____

Show your work on another sheet.
Write your answers here.

Total Problems	30
Problems Correct	_____

1. 436
× 28

2. 327
× 51

3. 824
× 32

4. 528
× 63

5. 232
× 82

6. 329
× 18

7. 252
× 45

8. 362
× 54

9. 243
× 84

10. 392
× 41

11. 354
× 25

12. 236
× 57

13. 583
× 32

14. 442
× 23

15. 623
× 52

16. 542
× 78

17. 825
× 43

18. 514
× 62

19. 362
× 54

20. 424
× 49

21. 282
× 91

22. 989
× 22

23. 418
× 35

24. 683
× 83

25. 536
× 24

26. 817
× 53

27. 724
× 46

Success ahoy! Just practice!

28. 325
× 72

29. 824
× 56

30. 633
× 38

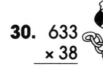

Multiplication

Name _____

Show your work on another sheet.
Write your answers here.

Total Problems	30
Problems Correct	_____

1. 324
× 213

2. 212
× 525

3. 232
× 314

4. 213
× 243

5. 123
× 423

6. 415
× 324

7. 234
× 523

8. 324
× 221

9. 312
× 356

10. 524
× 412

11. 132
× 623

12. 253
× 414

13. 543
× 231

14. 213
× 536

15. 134
× 821

16. 242
× 325

17. 136
× 523

18. 452
× 145

19. 143
× 632

20. 813
× 231

21. 325
× 462

22. 234
× 241

23. 721
× 325

24. 232
× 465

25. 124
× 532

26. 141
× 282

27. 214
× 625

28. 243
× 312

29. 224
× 431

30. 213
× 189

Practice = Success!

 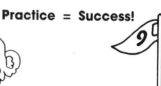

Division

Name _____

Total Problems ___31___

Problems Correct _____

1.
4)12

2.
3)15

3.
2)18

4.
6)24

5.
3)21

6.
5)25

7.
4)16

8.
5)20

9.
7)14

10.
8)8

11.
4)32

12.
6)30

13.
3)27

14.
8)16

15.
8)24

16.
9)18

17.
4)24

18.
5)5

19.
7)28

20.
1)5

21.
4)36

22.
1)9

23.
7)21

24.
5)15

25.
9)36

26.
3)24

27.
8)32

With practice, you can do it!

28.
5)30

29.
3)18

30.
9)27

31.
5)35

Division

Name _____

Total Problems	32
Problems Correct	_____

1.
8) 48

2.
4) 32

3.
6) 36

4.
7) 42

5.
4) 28

6.
9) 45

7.
8) 56

8.
6) 30

9.
9) 54

10.
7) 49

11.
5) 35

12.
6) 24

13.
9) 36

14.
8) 40

15.
9) 63

16.
7) 21

17.
6) 54

18.
4) 20

19.
8) 32

20.
7) 56

21.
3) 21

22.
5) 40

23.
5) 20

24.
5) 45

25.
6) 42

26.
7) 35

27.
7) 28

Practice = Success!

28.
6) 48

29.
4) 24

30.
7) 63

31.
5) 30

32.
4) 36

Division

Name _____

Total Problems	32
Problems Correct	_____

1. 6)48

2. 7)28

3. 7)42

4. 8)56

5. 6)24

6. 5)35

7. 8)64

8. 6)30

9. 9)63

10. 7)49

11. 8)40

12. 9)54

13. 4)32

14. 5)45

15. 7)56

16. 4)36

17. 5)30

18. 7)63

19. 8)72

20. 7)35

21. 5)40

22. 9)81

23. 4)28

24. 4)24

25. 6)54

26. 6)36

27. 9)72

28. 8)48

29. 9)36

30. 6)42

31. 9)45

32. 8)32

Division

Name _____

Total Problems	32
Problems Correct	_____

1.
3⟌15

2.
8⟌40

3.
3⟌21

4.
9⟌36

5.
4⟌20

6.
8⟌32

7.
9⟌9

8.
5⟌35

9.
9⟌81

10.
6⟌36

11.
4⟌32

12.
8⟌64

13.
1⟌4

14.
7⟌42

15.
7⟌28

16.
6⟌30

17.
3⟌24

18.
6⟌48

19.
9⟌54

20.
3⟌18

21.
8⟌72

22.
6⟌24

23.
8⟌56

24.
7⟌35

25.
4⟌28

26.
7⟌49

27.
6⟌54

Practice! Practice! Practice!

28.
8⟌48

29.
5⟌45

30.
9⟌72

31.
3⟌27

32.
7⟌7

Division

Name _____

Total Problems _____38_____

Problems Correct _____

1. 5⟌30

2. 7⟌21

3. 4⟌28

4. 9⟌63

5. 5⟌35

6. 1⟌9

7. 4⟌24

8. 8⟌32

9. 6⟌36

10. 2⟌14

11. 7⟌56

12. 4⟌36

13. 9⟌27

14. 6⟌42

15. 8⟌8

16. 3⟌24

17. 7⟌63

18. 9⟌54

19. 3⟌27

20. 1⟌7

21. 8⟌24

22. 2⟌16

23. 7⟌42

24. 6⟌54

25. 8⟌56

26. 4⟌32

27. 9⟌72

28. 5⟌45

29. 3⟌21

30. 8⟌64

31. 5⟌45

32. 7⟌49

33. 9⟌54

34. 3⟌36

35. 8⟌72

Practice hard. You'll win!

36. 7⟌28

37. 5⟌40

38. 6⟌30

Division

Name _____

Total Problems	30
Problems Correct	___

1. ___ R
4⟌17

2. ___ R
3⟌22

3. ___ R
4⟌21

4. ___ R
3⟌29

5. ___ R
4⟌26

6. ___ R
8⟌34

7. ___ R
8⟌27

8. ___ R
4⟌30

9. ___ R
7⟌23

10. ___ R
5⟌32

11. ___ R
3⟌26

12. ___ R
5⟌38

13. ___ R
3⟌20

14. ___ R
4⟌37

15. ___ R
9⟌38

16. ___ R
6⟌21

17. ___ R
5⟌42

18. ___ R
5⟌26

19. ___ R
4⟌35

20. ___ R
2⟌15

21. ___ R
7⟌29

22. ___ R
9⟌48

23. ___ R
5⟌22

24. ___ R
9⟌28

25. ___ R
6⟌34

26. ___ R
5⟌47

27. ___ R
6⟌15

28. ___ R
8⟌44

29. ___ R
6⟌27

30. ___ R
7⟌37

**Practice puts
you on top!**

Division

Name _____

Total Problems	30
Problems Correct	_____

1. ____ R
6 | 44

2. ____ R
9 | 83

3. ____ R
8 | 49

4. ____ R
6 | 40

5. ____ R
8 | 57

6. ____ R
6 | 50

7. ____ R
9 | 47

8. ____ R
5 | 42

9. ____ R
8 | 65

10. ____ R
7 | 37

11. ____ R
9 | 56

12. ____ R
4 | 37

13. ____ R
7 | 58

14. ____ R
5 | 34

15. ____ R
9 | 64

16. ____ R
6 | 57

17. ____ R
8 | 33

18. ____ R
7 | 53

19. ____ R
9 | 74

20. ____ R
4 | 29

21. ____ R
8 | 73

22. ____ R
5 | 46

23. ____ R
7 | 45

24. ____ R
7 | 65

25. ____ R
8 | 41

26. ____ R
5 | 36

Practice hard. You'll win!

27. ____ R
9 | 38

28. ____ R
4 | 34

29. ____ R
7 | 30

30. ____ R
6 | 32

Math IF8740

72

Division

Name _____

Total Problems	30
Problems Correct	_____

1. _____ R
5$\overline{)21}$

2. _____ R
3$\overline{)22}$

3. _____ R
3$\overline{)19}$

4. _____ R
4$\overline{)18}$

5. _____ R
5$\overline{)27}$

6. _____ R
8$\overline{)41}$

7. _____ R
4$\overline{)34}$

8. _____ R
7$\overline{)51}$

9. _____ R
7$\overline{)43}$

10. _____ R
8$\overline{)65}$

11. _____ R
6$\overline{)19}$

12. _____ R
3$\overline{)26}$

13. _____ R
2$\overline{)19}$

14. _____ R
8$\overline{)57}$

15. _____ R
6$\overline{)49}$

16. _____ R
2$\overline{)17}$

17. _____ R
3$\overline{)29}$

18. _____ R
5$\overline{)32}$

19. _____ R
9$\overline{)83}$

20. _____ R
6$\overline{)44}$

21. _____ R
5$\overline{)47}$

22. _____ R
6$\overline{)38}$

23. _____ R
2$\overline{)13}$

24. _____ R
5$\overline{)16}$

25. _____ R
3$\overline{)20}$

26. _____ R
9$\overline{)64}$

27. _____ R
8$\overline{)51}$

28. _____ R
8$\overline{)73}$

29. _____ R
5$\overline{)43}$

30. _____ R
7$\overline{)68}$

With practice, you can do it!

Division

Name _____

Show your work on another sheet.
Write your answers here.

Total Problems	32
Problems Correct	_____

1.
$7 \overline{)30}$

2.
$8 \overline{)43}$

3.
$9 \overline{)75}$

4.
$6 \overline{)26}$

5.
$5 \overline{)27}$

6.
$8 \overline{)26}$

7.
$6 \overline{)52}$

8.
$9 \overline{)39}$

9.
$4 \overline{)34}$

10.
$9 \overline{)48}$

11.
$7 \overline{)38}$

12.
$3 \overline{)22}$

13.
$5 \overline{)37}$

14.
$6 \overline{)38}$

15.
$6 \overline{)33}$

16.
$3 \overline{)26}$

17.
$8 \overline{)58}$

18.
$7 \overline{)51}$

19.
$9 \overline{)84}$

20.
$4 \overline{)30}$

21.
$4 \overline{)22}$

22.
$9 \overline{)64}$

23.
$6 \overline{)45}$

24.
$8 \overline{)66}$

25.
$7 \overline{)65}$

26.
$2 \overline{)19}$

27.
$2 \overline{)17}$

28.
$8 \overline{)34}$

29.
$5 \overline{)28}$

Practice makes perfect!

30.
$9 \overline{)57}$

31.
$7 \overline{)24}$

32.
$3 \overline{)29}$

Division

Name _____

Show your work on another sheet.
Write your answers here.

Total Problems	__32__
Problems Correct	_____

1.
8 ⟌ 74

2.
5 ⟌ 32

3.
6 ⟌ 50

4.
3 ⟌ 20

5.
9 ⟌ 50

6.
7 ⟌ 59

7.
4 ⟌ 38

8.
8 ⟌ 50

9.
4 ⟌ 27

10.
9 ⟌ 47

11.
8 ⟌ 61

12.
7 ⟌ 40

13.
6 ⟌ 57

14.
9 ⟌ 82

15.
2 ⟌ 11

16.
7 ⟌ 48

17.
9 ⟌ 73

18.
5 ⟌ 47

19.
6 ⟌ 44

20.
7 ⟌ 68

21.
3 ⟌ 17

22.
8 ⟌ 47

23.
6 ⟌ 31

24.
5 ⟌ 43

25.
9 ⟌ 87

26.
3 ⟌ 28

27.
6 ⟌ 20

28.
9 ⟌ 38

29.
2 ⟌ 13

Practice! Practice! Practice!

30.
7 ⟌ 27

31.
8 ⟌ 39

32.
4 ⟌ 35

© 1990 Instructional Fair, Inc.

Division

Name _____

Show your work on another sheet.
Write your answers here.

Total Problems	__32__
Problems Correct	_____

1.
2 | 46

2.
3 | 93

3.
4 | 84

4.
9 | 90

5.
2 | 68

6.
7 | 77

7.
4 | 48

8.
3 | 63

9.
8 | 88

10.
2 | 24

11.
3 | 36

12.
5 | 50

13.
6 | 60

14.
2 | 64

15.
4 | 44

16.
2 | 28

17.
3 | 99

18.
2 | 66

19.
2 | 62

20.
3 | 69

21.
2 | 82

22.
6 | 66

23.
2 | 48

24.
3 | 39

25.
9 | 99

26.
2 | 84

27.
5 | 55

28.
8 | 80

29.
2 | 86

With practice, you can do it!

30.
2 | 26

31.
7 | 70

32.
3 | 96

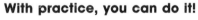

Division

Name _____

Show your work on another sheet.
Write your answers here.

Total Problems	32
Problems Correct	_____

1.
3)68

2.
3)86

3.
2)47

4.
5)57

5.
8)89

6.
3)95

7.
7)79

8.
2)65

9.
4)87

10.
3)37

11.
5)59

12.
2)87

13.
4)45

14.
3)64

15.
2)83

16.
8)97

17.
6)79

18.
4)65

19.
7)95

20.
3)74

21.
5)72

22.
2)53

23.
7)86

24.
3)47

25.
6)81

26.
4)53

27.
8)98

28.
3)55

29.
6)75

Success ahoy! Just practice!

30.
4)71

31.
2)35

32.
5)93

Division

Name _____

Show your work on another sheet.
Write your answers here.

| Total Problems | __32__ |
| Problems Correct | _____ |

1.
6$\overline{)92}$

2.
4$\overline{)63}$

3.
2$\overline{)37}$

4.
7$\overline{)96}$

5.
3$\overline{)56}$

6.
5$\overline{)63}$

7.
8$\overline{)99}$

8.
4$\overline{)55}$

9.
6$\overline{)85}$

10.
5$\overline{)74}$

11.
2$\overline{)75}$

12.
4$\overline{)95}$

13.
7$\overline{)82}$

14.
3$\overline{)85}$

15.
8$\overline{)95}$

16.
4$\overline{)75}$

17.
5$\overline{)82}$

18.
3$\overline{)77}$

19.
6$\overline{)89}$

20.
2$\overline{)57}$

21.
7$\overline{)93}$

22.
5$\overline{)74}$

23.
2$\overline{)93}$

24.
4$\overline{)67}$

25.
3$\overline{)43}$

26.
6$\overline{)95}$

27.
2$\overline{)77}$

28.
8$\overline{)93}$

29.
3$\overline{)58}$

30.
5$\overline{)94}$

31.
7$\overline{)85}$

32.
6$\overline{)71}$

Practice = Success!

Division

Name _____

Show your work on another sheet.
Write your answers here.

Total Problems	27
Problems Correct	_____

1.
$3\overline{)225}$

2.
$6\overline{)324}$

3.
$9\overline{)288}$

4.
$2\overline{)138}$

5.
$7\overline{)455}$

6.
$4\overline{)216}$

7.
$8\overline{)504}$

8.
$5\overline{)270}$

9.
$3\overline{)171}$

10.
$6\overline{)378}$

11.
$9\overline{)855}$

12.
$2\overline{)194}$

13.
$7\overline{)385}$

14.
$4\overline{)304}$

15.
$5\overline{)435}$

16.
$3\overline{)201}$

17.
$6\overline{)348}$

18.
$8\overline{)744}$

19.
$2\overline{)154}$

20.
$9\overline{)306}$

21.
$4\overline{)224}$

22.
$7\overline{)644}$

Practice hard. You'll win!

23.
$5\overline{)475}$

24.
$3\overline{)282}$

25.
$6\overline{)588}$

26.
$9\overline{)252}$

27.
$2\overline{)176}$

Division

Name _____

Show your work on another sheet.
Write your answers here.

Total Problems	32
Problems Correct	_____

1.
2) 155

2.
4) 358

3.
6) 273

4.
8) 428

5.
9) 399

6.
3) 296

7.
5) 291

8.
7) 549

9.
2) 173

10.
5) 439

11.
9) 758

12.
6) 392

13.
7) 279

14.
3) 209

15.
4) 231

16.
8) 699

17.
2) 119

18.
6) 507

19.
5) 197

20.
9) 479

21.
3) 173

22.
7) 408

23.
6) 237

24.
5) 338

25.
4) 314

26.
8) 389

27.
9) 245

28.
5) 238

29.
2) 137

**Practice hard.
You'll win!**

30.
3) 295

31.
8) 597

32.
6) 319

Math IF8740

© 1990 Instructional Fair, Inc.

Division

Show your work on another sheet.
Write your answers here.

Total Problems ___27___

Problems Correct _____

1.
8 | 532

2.
4 | 269

3.
6 | 562

4.
2 | 179

5.
9 | 659

6.
3 | 119

7.
7 | 439

8.
5 | 484

9.
4 | 155

10.
9 | 587

11.
8 | 757

12.
2 | 157

13.
3 | 143

14.
6 | 338

15.
2 | 193

16.
7 | 331

17.
9 | 291

18.
8 | 210

19.
4 | 383

20.
3 | 224

21.
5 | 374

22.
6 | 537

23.
9 | 867

24.
2 | 135

25.
6 | 446

26.
3 | 254

27.
8 | 307

Practice! Practice! Practice!

Division

Show your work on another sheet.
Write your answers here.

Total Problems ____27____

Problems Correct _____

1.
2 | 432

2.
4 | 924

3.
6 | 726

4.
5 | 575

5.
3 | 456

6.
7 | 784

7.
9 | 999

8.
8 | 896

9.
4 | 848

10.
2 | 952

11.
5 | 715

12.
3 | 942

13.
6 | 786

14.
5 | 765

15.
4 | 932

16.
3 | 759

17.
2 | 726

18.
5 | 585

19.
7 | 784

20.
2 | 548

21.
6 | 972

22.
4 | 968

23.
2 | 746

24.
8 | 896

25.
4 | 856

Through practice you learn!

26.
3 | 945

27.
7 | 854

Division

Name _____

Show your work on another sheet.
Write your answers here.

Total Problems _____27_____

Problems Correct _____

1.
2$\overline{)437}$

2.
6$\overline{)739}$

3.
4$\overline{)979}$

4.
5$\overline{)994}$

5.
3$\overline{)596}$

6.
8$\overline{)899}$

7.
7$\overline{)804}$

8.
6$\overline{)879}$

9.
5$\overline{)734}$

10.
2$\overline{)753}$

11.
4$\overline{)595}$

12.
3$\overline{)748}$

13.
7$\overline{)978}$

14.
6$\overline{)887}$

15.
4$\overline{)759}$

16.
2$\overline{)537}$

17.
5$\overline{)687}$

18.
8$\overline{)897}$

19.
4$\overline{)635}$

20.
3$\overline{)836}$

21.
6$\overline{)689}$

22.
2$\overline{)379}$

23.
5$\overline{)748}$

24.
8$\overline{)907}$

25.
6$\overline{)987}$

Practice brings success!

26.
7$\overline{)858}$

27.
4$\overline{)675}$

Division

Name _____

Show your work on another sheet.
Write your answers here.

Total Problems	__27__
Problems Correct	_____

1.
3)‾746‾

2.
7)‾796‾

3.
5)‾893‾

4.
4)‾943‾

5.
6)‾676‾

6.
8)‾978‾

7.
2)‾337‾

8.
7)‾957‾

9.
3)‾446‾

10.
4)‾538‾

11.
6)‾759‾

12.
5)‾684‾

13.
8)‾894‾

14.
2)‾487‾

15.
3)‾953‾

16.
6)‾945‾

17.
4)‾629‾

18.
7)‾879‾

19.
5)‾947‾

20.
2)‾951‾

21.
4)‾739‾

22.
3)‾647‾

23.
6)‾857‾

24.
2)‾859‾

25.
4)‾938‾

Practice = Success!

26.
3)‾773‾

27.
5)‾817‾

Division

Name _____

Show your work on another sheet.
Write your answers here.

Total Problems	__27__
Problems Correct	_____

1.
6)65

2.
9)94

3.
3)925

4.
7)564

5.
4)823

6.
5)253

7.
8)865

8.
2)841

9.
7)75

10.
6)364

11.
4)414

12.
5)404

13.
8)327

14.
3)623

15.
2)461

16.
7)423

17.
6)627

18.
5)529

19.
4)842

20.
3)961

21.
8)325

22.
7)738

23.
6)423

24.
2)241

25.
5)539

Success ahoy! Just practice!

26.
3)272

27.
4)83

Division

Name _____

Show your work on another sheet.
Write your answers here.

Total Problems	27
Problems Correct	_____

1.
8⟌87

2.
5⟌53

3.
4⟌842

4.
7⟌426

5.
3⟌92

6.
6⟌484

7.
8⟌839

8.
2⟌615

9.
9⟌98

10.
6⟌543

11.
7⟌73

12.
4⟌483

13.
3⟌272

14.
5⟌517

15.
7⟌634

16.
2⟌815

17.
6⟌364

18.
4⟌323

19.
8⟌726

20.
3⟌631

21.
6⟌632

22.
5⟌453

23.
7⟌738

24.
2⟌421

25.
9⟌938

Practice brings success!

26.
5⟌526

27.
4⟌283

Division

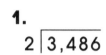

Name _____

Show your work on another sheet.
Write your answers here.

Total Problems	27
Problems Correct	_____

1.
2)‾3,486

2.
4)‾8,572

3.
6)‾3,764

4.
5)‾5,328

5.
3)‾2,874

6.
2)‾8,497

7.
7)‾8,598

8.
2)‾8,040

9.
4)‾2,988

10.
6)‾8,149

11.
7)‾5,001

12.
3)‾6,238

13.
5)‾7,384

14.
8)‾4,376

15.
2)‾4,811

16.
4)‾1,583

17.
6)‾7,391

18.
3)‾6,943

19.
7)‾4,795

20.
5)‾5,237

21.
8)‾4,687

22.
2)‾6,841

23.
4)‾9,035

24.
6)‾9,469

25.
3)‾6,238

Practice hard. You'll win!

26.
9)‾2,819

27.
5)‾3,381

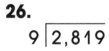

Division

Name _____

Show your work on another sheet.
Write your answers here.

Total Problems	27
Problems Correct	_____

1. 21$\overline{)64}$

2. 42$\overline{)93}$

3. 34$\overline{)74}$

4. 12$\overline{)75}$

5. 45$\overline{)96}$

6. 24$\overline{)82}$

7. 37$\overline{)86}$

8. 14$\overline{)73}$

9. 48$\overline{)97}$

10. 16$\overline{)69}$

11. 29$\overline{)93}$

12. 40$\overline{)87}$

13. 18$\overline{)61}$

14. 38$\overline{)83}$

15. 27$\overline{)82}$

16. 76$\overline{)94}$

17. 19$\overline{)88}$

18. 14$\overline{)85}$

19. 28$\overline{)96}$

20. 17$\overline{)73}$

21. 25$\overline{)61}$

22. 23$\overline{)70}$

23. 15$\overline{)84}$

24. 22$\overline{)90}$

25. 35$\overline{)81}$

Through practice you learn!

26. 13$\overline{)96}$

27. 18$\overline{)93}$

88

Division

Name _____

Show your work on another sheet.
Write your answers here.

Total Problems	27
Problems Correct	_____

1.
$34\overline{)214}$

2.
$63\overline{)569}$

3.
$81\overline{)490}$

4.
$23\overline{)172}$

5.
$15\overline{)131}$

6.
$37\overline{)192}$

7.
$24\overline{)205}$

8.
$78\overline{)475}$

9.
$92\overline{)473}$

10.
$46\overline{)382}$

11.
$67\overline{)432}$

12.
$21\overline{)153}$

13.
$32\overline{)270}$

14.
$86\overline{)803}$

15.
$74\overline{)456}$

16.
$31\overline{)261}$

17.
$65\overline{)421}$

18.
$41\overline{)306}$

19.
$68\overline{)641}$

20.
$38\overline{)320}$

21.
$28\overline{)262}$

22.
$49\overline{)321}$

23.
$79\overline{)665}$

24.
$27\overline{)171}$

25.
$83\overline{)597}$

Practice = Success!

26.
$34\overline{)327}$

27.
$58\overline{)312}$

Division

Name _____

Show your work on another sheet.
Write your answers here.

Total Problems	27
Problems Correct	_____

1.
14 | 1 3 2

2.
23 | 1 9 6

3.
64 | 5 8 8

4.
83 | 6 0 4

5.
76 | 6 4 3

6.
92 | 5 7 4

7.
17 | 1 1 0

8.
26 | 2 1 4

9.
37 | 1 9 4

10.
53 | 4 8 1

11.
47 | 2 9 7

12.
25 | 1 8 4

13.
73 | 4 5 1

14.
87 | 8 2 1

15.
24 | 2 0 7

16.
34 | 2 1 7

17.
67 | 2 8 5

18.
68 | 4 2 1

19.
71 | 6 5 8

20.
32 | 2 6 8

21.
29 | 2 0 7

22.
57 | 5 5 7

23.
35 | 2 5 8

24.
27 | 2 4 1

25.
62 | 4 3 0

Anything's possible with practice!

26.
52 | 3 8 1

27.
38 | 3 6 6

Division

Name _____

Show your work on another sheet.
Write your answers here.

Total Problems	__27__
Problems Correct	_____

1.
26 | 375

2.
17 | 366

3.
47 | 822

4.
84 | 927

5.
12 | 777

6.
36 | 915

7.
58 | 902

8.
91 | 952

9.
53 | 948

10.
32 | 847

11.
71 | 997

12.
68 | 868

13.
75 | 888

14.
41 | 886

15.
82 | 833

16.
18 | 822

17.
31 | 827

18.
19 | 777

19.
35 | 819

20.
46 | 821

21.
94 | 977

22.
77 | 970

23.
88 | 995

24.
38 | 971

25.
57 | 787

Practice and anything's possible!

26.
43 | 844

27.
67 | 973

Division

Name _____

Show your work on another sheet.
Write your answers here.

Total Problems	27
Problems Correct	_____

1.
17) 998

2.
23) 364

3.
49) 627

4.
36) 950

5.
72) 854

6.
26) 949

7.
14) 874

8.
32) 751

9.
56) 807

10.
13) 895

11.
29) 738

12.
46) 588

13.
24) 527

14.
42) 710

15.
73) 868

16.
39) 789

17.
27) 845

18.
15) 764

19.
34) 819

20.
25) 591

21.
18) 822

22.
53) 642

23.
12) 725

24.
38) 667

25.
51) 555

Practice hard. You'll win!

26.
29) 902

27.
19) 774

Division

Name _____

Show your work on another sheet.
Write your answers here.

1.
21 | 4,284

2.
40 | 8,040

3.
15 | 3,045

4.
25 | 5,025

5.
12 | 6,024

6.
13 | 2,743

7.
41 | 4,551

8.
17 | 1,904

9.
22 | 4,642

10.
31 | 9,641

11.
52 | 5,252

12.
10 | 3,370

13.
40 | 8,440

14.
11 | 6,853

15.
21 | 6,594

16.
32 | 9,984

17.
45 | 9,045

18.
10 | 4,680

19.
12 | 6,372

20.
35 | 7,735

21.
24 | 5,088

22.
14 | 1,428

Through practice you learn!

23.
61 | 6,771

24.
20 | 8,840

25.
32 | 6,752

Fractions

Name _____

Total Problems	28
Problems Correct	____

1. $\dfrac{2}{6} + \dfrac{1}{6}$

2. $\dfrac{3}{7} + \dfrac{2}{7}$

3. $\dfrac{1}{4} + \dfrac{2}{4}$

4. $\dfrac{3}{9} + \dfrac{4}{9}$

5. $\dfrac{4}{8} + \dfrac{2}{8}$

6. $\dfrac{1}{5} + \dfrac{3}{5}$

7. $\dfrac{3}{10} + \dfrac{6}{10}$

8. $\dfrac{4}{12} + \dfrac{6}{12}$

9. $\dfrac{2}{5} + \dfrac{3}{5}$

10. $\dfrac{4}{9} + \dfrac{4}{9}$

11. $\dfrac{5}{10} + \dfrac{2}{10}$

12. $\dfrac{4}{7} + \dfrac{1}{7}$

13. $\dfrac{1}{2} + \dfrac{1}{2}$

14. $\dfrac{5}{8} + \dfrac{2}{8}$

15. $\dfrac{3}{6} + \dfrac{1}{6}$

16. $\dfrac{6}{7} + \dfrac{1}{7}$

17. $\dfrac{4}{8} + \dfrac{4}{8}$

18. $\dfrac{2}{6} + \dfrac{2}{6}$

19. $\dfrac{1}{3} + \dfrac{2}{3}$

20. $\dfrac{2}{5} + \dfrac{2}{5}$

21. $\dfrac{5}{12} + \dfrac{3}{12}$

22. $\dfrac{5}{9} + \dfrac{3}{9}$

23. $\dfrac{2}{4} + \dfrac{2}{4}$

24. $\dfrac{7}{12} + \dfrac{3}{12}$

25. $\dfrac{1}{5} + \dfrac{4}{5}$

26. $\dfrac{2}{7} + \dfrac{4}{7}$

27. $\dfrac{3}{8} + \dfrac{4}{8}$

28. $\dfrac{2}{10} + \dfrac{3}{10}$

Practice! Practice! Practice!

Fractions

Name _____

Total Problems	28
Problems Correct	_____

1.
$$\frac{3}{6}$$
$$-\frac{1}{6}$$

2.
$$\frac{7}{8}$$
$$-\frac{5}{8}$$

3.
$$\frac{7}{10}$$
$$-\frac{4}{10}$$

4.
$$\frac{4}{4}$$
$$-\frac{3}{4}$$

5.
$$\frac{8}{9}$$
$$-\frac{4}{9}$$

6.
$$\frac{11}{12}$$
$$-\frac{5}{12}$$

7.
$$\frac{7}{9}$$
$$-\frac{5}{9}$$

8.
$$\frac{4}{5}$$
$$-\frac{2}{5}$$

9.
$$\frac{6}{7}$$
$$-\frac{4}{7}$$

10.
$$\frac{3}{5}$$
$$-\frac{2}{5}$$

11.
$$\frac{8}{8}$$
$$-\frac{5}{8}$$

12.
$$\frac{9}{9}$$
$$-\frac{2}{9}$$

13.
$$\frac{9}{10}$$
$$-\frac{7}{10}$$

14.
$$\frac{2}{2}$$
$$-\frac{1}{2}$$

15.
$$\frac{5}{6}$$
$$-\frac{4}{6}$$

16.
$$\frac{11}{12}$$
$$-\frac{8}{12}$$

17.
$$\frac{6}{6}$$
$$-\frac{2}{6}$$

18.
$$\frac{7}{8}$$
$$-\frac{7}{8}$$

19.
$$\frac{3}{4}$$
$$-\frac{1}{4}$$

20.
$$\frac{7}{7}$$
$$-\frac{4}{7}$$

21.
$$\frac{10}{12}$$
$$-\frac{6}{12}$$

22.
$$\frac{1}{2}$$
$$-\frac{1}{2}$$

23.
$$\frac{5}{5}$$
$$-\frac{1}{5}$$

**Anything's possible
with practice!**

24.
$$\frac{12}{12}$$
$$-\frac{8}{12}$$

25.
$$\frac{5}{9}$$
$$-\frac{3}{9}$$

26.
$$\frac{6}{10}$$
$$-\frac{4}{10}$$

27.
$$\frac{6}{6}$$
$$-\frac{3}{6}$$

28.
$$\frac{4}{7}$$
$$-\frac{1}{7}$$

Mixed Numerals   Name _____

Total Problems	25
Problems Correct	_____

1. $3\frac{2}{5}$
$+ 5\frac{1}{5}$

---

2. $4\frac{2}{6}$
$+ 5\frac{3}{6}$

3. $8\frac{1}{4}$
$+ 3\frac{2}{4}$

4. $3\frac{1}{5}$
$+ 9\frac{1}{5}$

5. $6\frac{3}{7}$
$+ 2\frac{2}{7}$

6. $8\frac{1}{9}$
$+ 3\frac{6}{9}$

7. $7\frac{2}{12}$
$+ 9\frac{3}{12}$

---

8. $5\frac{1}{3}$
$+ 7\frac{1}{3}$

9. $6\frac{1}{8}$
$+ 5\frac{2}{8}$

10. $4\frac{3}{7}$
$+ 9\frac{3}{7}$

11. $9\frac{1}{4}$
$+ 8\frac{2}{4}$

12. $7\frac{2}{5}$
$+ 3\frac{1}{5}$

13. $9\frac{3}{6}$
$+ 2\frac{1}{6}$

---

14. $4\frac{2}{9}$
$+ 6\frac{5}{9}$

15. $6\frac{4}{10}$
$+ 7\frac{5}{10}$

16. $6\frac{3}{8}$
$+ 9\frac{4}{8}$

17. $9\frac{5}{12}$
$+ 7\frac{6}{12}$

18. $7\frac{2}{8}$
$+ 7\frac{5}{8}$

19. $6\frac{5}{7}$
$+ 9\frac{1}{7}$

---

20. $9\frac{4}{7}$
$+ 8\frac{1}{7}$

21. $3\frac{2}{4}$
$+ 1\frac{1}{4}$

22. $8\frac{3}{10}$
$+ 5\frac{6}{10}$

Practice = Success!

---

23. $5\frac{3}{6}$
$+ 9\frac{2}{6}$

24. $7\frac{6}{12}$
$+ 8\frac{3}{12}$

25. $4\frac{3}{9}$
$+ 7\frac{4}{9}$

Mixed Numerals

Name _____

Total Problems	25
Problems Correct	_____

1. $9\frac{4}{6}$
$- 3\frac{2}{6}$

2. $14\frac{5}{9}$
$- 6\frac{2}{9}$

3. $7\frac{8}{10}$
$- 3\frac{4}{10}$

4. $13\frac{2}{7}$
$- 8\frac{1}{7}$

5. $10\frac{6}{8}$
$- 4\frac{2}{8}$

6. $11\frac{7}{12}$
$- 5\frac{3}{12}$

7. $8\frac{3}{4}$
$- 6\frac{1}{4}$

8. $12\frac{5}{8}$
$- 7\frac{3}{8}$

9. $8\frac{3}{5}$
$- 4\frac{1}{5}$

10. $9\frac{5}{6}$
$- 7\frac{4}{6}$

11. $17\frac{8}{9}$
$- 9\frac{3}{9}$

12. $8\frac{7}{10}$
$- 5\frac{3}{10}$

13. $12\frac{6}{7}$
$- 9\frac{4}{7}$

14. $11\frac{4}{5}$
$- 3\frac{2}{5}$

15. $10\frac{7}{9}$
$- 6\frac{4}{9}$

16. $16\frac{7}{8}$
$- 7\frac{4}{8}$

17. $13\frac{9}{10}$
$- 7\frac{4}{10}$

18. $11\frac{10}{12}$
$- 8\frac{4}{12}$

19. $12\frac{6}{6}$
$- 5\frac{2}{6}$

20. $18\frac{6}{7}$
$- 9\frac{1}{7}$

21. $15\frac{10}{10}$
$- 8\frac{6}{10}$

22. $7\frac{11}{12}$
$- 4\frac{9}{12}$

Practice makes perfect!

23. $9\frac{4}{6}$
$- 2\frac{3}{6}$

24. $6\frac{4}{7}$
$- 2\frac{1}{7}$

25. $8\frac{5}{5}$
$- 3\frac{1}{5}$

Decimals

Name _____

Total Problems	30
Problems Correct	_____

1. 0.74
  + 0.69

2. 0.46
  + 0.98

3. 6.5
  + 4.8

4. 9.7
  + 8.8

5. 7.32
  + 3.49

6. 4.65
  + 9.27

7. 9.32
  + 5.29

8. 5.36
  + 6.78

9. 71.54
  + 5.76

10. 84.68
  + 7.43

11. 27.99
  + 8.43

12. 64.87
  + 5.43

13. 8.45
  + 43.86

14. 9.63
  + 62.49

15. 34.65
  + 25.87

16. 54.65
  + 38.75

17. 75.46
  + 48.37

18. 32.49
  + 37.86

19. 65.42
  + 83.79

20. 24.30
  + 87.98

21. 37.45
  + 18.93

22. 84.32
  + 38.49

23. 79.43
  + 40.34

24. 54.75
  + 83.49

25. 64.32
  + 62.89

26. 94.36
  + 43.98

27. 48.32
  + 85.29

28. 84.35
  + 29.46

29. 76.45
  + 55.83

30. 24.89
  + 96.49

**Practice hard.
You'll win!**

Decimals

Name _____

Total Problems	30
Problems Correct	_____

1.   8.04
     0.63
   + 3.24

2.   5.43
     0.26
   + 6.52

3.   9.74
     0.43
   + 0.65

4.   5.40
     0.38
   + 0.29

5.   6.34
     0.48
   + 5.53

6.   0.46
     0.38
   + 6.25

7.   3.24
     2.85
   + 6.34

8.   5.36
     2.48
   + 6.53

9.   7.42
     3.85
   + 4.28

10.   2.41
     3.25
   + 1.38

11.   5.43
     2.51
   + 8.25

12.   8.45
     6.32
   + 2.58

13.   6.84
     7.35
   + 1.24

14.   3.24
     8.31
   + 2.56

15.   6.43
     1.32
   + 7.58

16. 65.42
     3.71
   + 4.28

17. 92.30
     4.64
   + 5.18

18. 84.35
     3.24
   + 4.93

19. 38.48
     2.35
   + 3.13

20. 64.35
     5.48
   + 2.83

21. 54.32
    63.85
   + 2.14

22. 74.35
    65.86
   + 3.44

23. 34.65
     2.87
  + 85.24

24. 72.45
     3.86
  + 94.47

25.   6.52
   43.69
  + 32.34

26.   5.48
   62.54
  + 38.62

27. 42.66
   34.87
  + 58.32

28. 84.32
   20.14
  + 83.23

29. 36.45
   72.59
  + 24.31

30. 74.32
   24.04
  + 15.21

Practice!
Practice!
Practice!

Decimals

Name _____

Total Problems	30
Problems Correct	_____

1. 0.65
    − 0.38

2. 0.92
    − 0.36

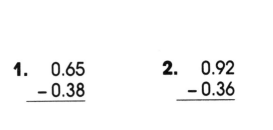

3. 0.53
    − 0.47

4. 9.42
    − 3.68

5. 6.45
    − 2.58

6. 7.52
    − 4.87

7. 5.71
    − 3.94

8. 9.25
    − 7.47

9. 8.82
    − 4.95

10. 3.45
    − 2.57

11. 7.45
    − 2.58

12. 6.45
    − 2.97

13. 35.21
    − 7.15

14. 68.45
    − 9.82

15. 52.38
    − 1.19

16. 87.45
    − 9.58

17. 74.38
    − 6.49

18. 47.36
    − 8.48

19. 96.45
    − 8.26

20. 72.40
    − 5.28

21. 35.46
    − 7.28

22. 66.41
    − 9.25

23. 32.45
    − 18.28

24. 65.48
    − 42.59

25. 98.45
    − 54.28

26. 74.36
    − 51.48

27. 51.42
    − 23.76

28. 29.43
    − 17.28

29. 86.45
    − 72.56

30. 72.48
    − 27.39

Practice hard. You'll win.

Decimals

Name _____

Total Problems _____30_____

Problems Correct _____

1. 0.28
× 3

2. 0.49
× 6

3. 0.43
× 9

4. 0.89
× 2

5. 0.57
× 4

6. 0.34
× 7

7. 0.86
× 5

8. 0.57
× 6

9. 0.98
× 3

10. 0.24
× 9

11. 0.53
× 8

12. 0.93
× 4

13. 0.65
× 7

14. 0.48
× 5

15. 0.96
× 2

16. 4.35
× 6

17. 2.31
× 9

18. 6.24
× 4

19. 7.34
× 3

20. 9.32
× 6

21. 8.76
× 2

22. 4.36
× 8

23. 5.49
× 7

24. 8.47
× 5

25. 6.58
× 4

26. 9.27
× 3

27. 4.39
× 6

28. 6.23
× 9

29. 8.76
× 2

30. 4.25
× 5

Practice!
Practice!
Practice!

Decimals

Name _____

Total Problems	30
Problems Correct	_____

1. 4.36
× 7

2. 0.48
× 9

3. 5.86
× 4

4. 0.97
× 3

5. 46.31
× 2

6. 32.44
× 3

7. 42.56
× 6

8. 52.38
× 5

9. 24.65
× 8

10. 47.68
× 9

11. 65.84
× 4

12. 37.45
× 7

13. 42.35
× 6

14. 98.37
× 2

15. 30.25
× 4

16. 84.27
× 3

17. 36.48
× 5

18. 24.07
× 9

19. 65.48
× 7

20. 37.42
× 8

21. 94.35
× 2

22. 43.48
× 6

23. 52.62
× 4

24. 97.45
× 3

25. 64.05
× 7

26. 84.36
× 5

27. 81.97
× 2

With practice, you can do it!

28. 70.46
× 6

29. 47.23
× 8

30. 24.57
× 9

Answer Key

Page 1

Addition

Name _____

Total Problems __35__

Problems Correct _____

1. 1 + 2 = 3
2. 4 + 7 = 11
3. 9 + 2 = 11
4. 4 + 1 = 5
5. 2 + 0 = 2
6. 3 + 5 = 8
7. 1 + 3 = 4
8. 4 + 4 = 8
9. 5 + 2 = 7
10. 3 + 3 = 6
11. 6 + 3 = 9
12. 2 + 3 = 5
13. 4 + 2 = 6
14. 6 + 2 = 8
15. 4 + 0 = 4
16. 7 + 3 = 10
17. 2 + 4 = 6
18. 2 + 7 = 9
19. 5 + 4 = 9
20. 3 + 0 = 3
21. 2 + 1 = 3
22. 8 + 3 = 11
23. 3 + 4 = 7
24. 2 + 5 = 7
25. 4 + 3 = 7
26. 2 + 9 = 11
27. 7 + 4 = 11
28. 3 + 2 = 5
29. 3 + 7 = 10
30. 8 + 2 = 10
31. 4 + 6 = 10
32. 4 + 9 = 13
33. 2 + 2 = 4
34. 4 + 8 = 12
35. 9 + 3 = 12

Practice = Success!

Page 1

Page 2

Addition

Name _____

Total Problems __35__

Problems Correct _____

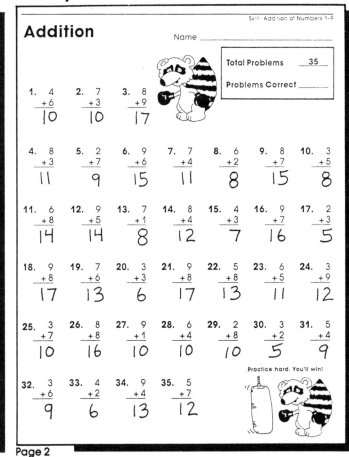

1. 4 + 6 = 10
2. 7 + 3 = 10
3. 8 + 9 = 17
4. 8 + 3 = 11
5. 2 + 7 = 9
6. 9 + 6 = 15
7. 7 + 4 = 11
8. 6 + 2 = 8
9. 8 + 7 = 15
10. 3 + 5 = 8
11. 6 + 8 = 14
12. 9 + 5 = 14
13. 7 + 1 = 8
14. 8 + 4 = 12
15. 4 + 3 = 7
16. 9 + 7 = 16
17. 2 + 3 = 5
18. 9 + 8 = 17
19. 7 + 6 = 13
20. 3 + 3 = 6
21. 9 + 8 = 17
22. 5 + 8 = 13
23. 6 + 5 = 11
24. 3 + 9 = 12
25. 3 + 7 = 10
26. 8 + 8 = 16
27. 9 + 1 = 10
28. 6 + 4 = 10
29. 2 + 8 = 10
30. 3 + 2 = 5
31. 5 + 4 = 9
32. 3 + 6 = 9
33. 4 + 2 = 6
34. 9 + 4 = 13
35. 5 + 7 = 12

Practice hard. You'll win!

Page 2

Page 3

Addition

Name _____

Total Problems __30__

Problems Correct _____

1. 34 + 52 = 86
2. 61 + 27 = 88
3. 84 + 14 = 98
4. 74 + 25 = 99
5. 56 + 33 = 89
6. 27 + 42 = 69
7. 65 + 21 = 86
8. 86 + 13 = 99
9. 43 + 25 = 68
10. 63 + 26 = 89
11. 37 + 45 = 82
12. 69 + 23 = 92
13. 25 + 79 = 104
14. 34 + 68 = 102
15. 56 + 37 = 93
16. 28 + 49 = 77
17. 36 + 25 = 61
18. 47 + 59 = 106
19. 78 + 16 = 94
20. 58 + 27 = 85
21. 38 + 97 = 135
22. 64 + 86 = 150
23. 95 + 67 = 162
24. 85 + 46 = 131
25. 74 + 39 = 113
26. 68 + 75 = 143
27. 57 + 83 = 140
28. 64 + 79 = 143
29. 96 + 25 = 121
30. 89 + 43 = 132

Practice and anything's possible!

Page 3

Page 4

Addition

Name _____

Total Problems __25__

Problems Correct _____

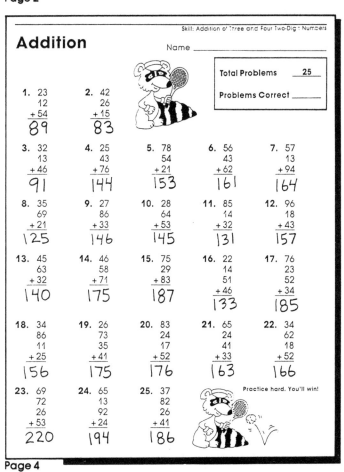

1. 23 + 12 + 54 = 89
2. 42 + 26 + 15 = 83
3. 32 + 13 + 46 = 91
4. 25 + 43 + 76 = 144
5. 78 + 54 + 21 = 153
6. 56 + 43 + 62 = 161
7. 57 + 13 + 94 = 164
8. 35 + 69 + 21 = 125
9. 27 + 86 + 33 = 146
10. 28 + 64 + 53 = 145
11. 85 + 14 + 32 = 131
12. 96 + 18 + 43 = 157
13. 45 + 63 + 32 = 140
14. 46 + 58 + 71 = 175
15. 75 + 29 + 83 = 187
16. 22 + 14 + 51 + 46 = 133
17. 76 + 23 + 52 + 34 = 185
18. 34 + 86 + 11 + 25 = 156
19. 26 + 73 + 35 + 41 = 175
20. 83 + 24 + 17 + 52 = 176
21. 65 + 24 + 41 + 33 = 163
22. 34 + 62 + 18 + 52 = 166
23. 69 + 72 + 26 + 53 = 220
24. 65 + 13 + 92 + 24 = 194
25. 37 + 82 + 26 + 41 = 186

Practice hard. You'll win!

Page 4

Answer Key

Addition

Name _____

Total Problems _____ 30
Problems Correct _____

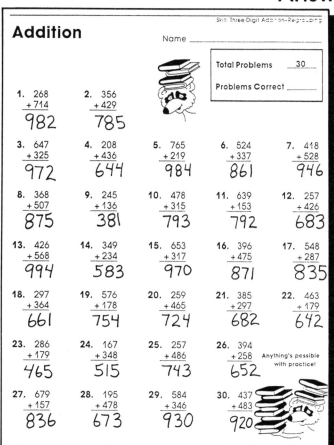

1. 268
   + 714
   982

2. 356
   + 429
   785

3. 647
   + 325
   972

4. 208
   + 436
   644

5. 765
   + 219
   984

6. 524
   + 337
   861

7. 418
   + 528
   946

8. 368
   + 507
   875

9. 245
   + 136
   381

10. 478
    + 315
    793

11. 639
    + 153
    792

12. 257
    + 426
    683

13. 426
    + 568
    994

14. 349
    + 234
    583

15. 653
    + 317
    970

16. 396
    + 475
    871

17. 548
    + 287
    835

18. 297
    + 364
    661

19. 576
    + 178
    754

20. 259
    + 465
    724

21. 385
    + 297
    682

22. 463
    + 179
    642

23. 286
    + 179
    465

24. 167
    + 348
    515

25. 257
    + 486
    743

26. 394
    + 258
    652   Anything's possible with practice!

27. 679
    + 157
    836

28. 195
    + 478
    673

29. 584
    + 346
    930

30. 437
    + 483
    920

Page 5

Addition

Name _____

Total Problems _____ 30
Problems Correct _____

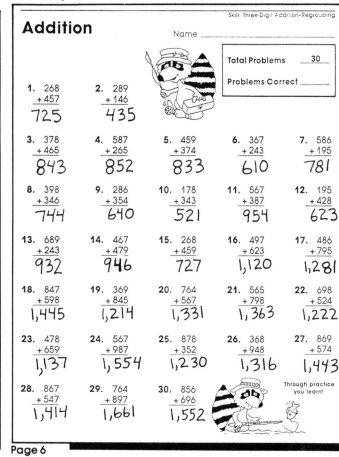

1. 268
   + 457
   725

2. 289
   + 146
   435

3. 378
   + 465
   843

4. 587
   + 265
   852

5. 459
   + 374
   833

6. 367
   + 243
   610

7. 586
   + 195
   781

8. 398
   + 346
   744

9. 286
   + 354
   640

10. 178
    + 343
    521

11. 567
    + 387
    954

12. 195
    + 428
    623

13. 689
    + 243
    932

14. 467
    + 479
    946

15. 268
    + 459
    727

16. 497
    + 623
    1,120

17. 486
    + 795
    1,281

18. 847
    + 598
    1,445

19. 369
    + 845
    1,214

20. 764
    + 567
    1,331

21. 565
    + 798
    1,363

22. 698
    + 524
    1,222

23. 478
    + 659
    1,137

24. 567
    + 987
    1,554

25. 878
    + 352
    1,230

26. 368
    + 948
    1,316

27. 869
    + 574
    1,443

28. 867
    + 547
    1,414

29. 764
    + 897
    1,661

30. 856
    + 696
    1,552

Through practice you learn!

Page 6

Addition

Name _____

Total Problems _____ 32
Problems Correct _____

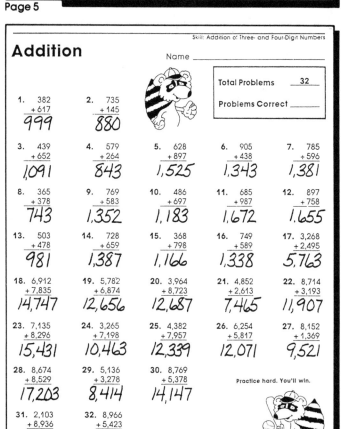

1. 382
   + 617
   999

2. 735
   + 145
   880

3. 439
   + 652
   1,091

4. 579
   + 264
   843

5. 628
   + 897
   1,525

6. 905
   + 438
   1,343

7. 785
   + 596
   1,381

8. 365
   + 378
   743

9. 769
   + 583
   1,352

10. 486
    + 697
    1,183

11. 685
    + 987
    1,672

12. 897
    + 758
    1,655

13. 503
    + 478
    981

14. 728
    + 659
    1,387

15. 368
    + 798
    1,166

16. 749
    + 589
    1,338

17. 3,268
    + 2,495
    5,763

18. 6,912
    + 7,835
    14,747

19. 5,782
    + 6,874
    12,656

20. 3,964
    + 8,723
    12,687

21. 4,852
    + 2,613
    7,465

22. 8,714
    + 3,193
    11,907

23. 7,135
    + 8,296
    15,431

24. 3,265
    + 7,198
    10,463

25. 4,382
    + 7,957
    12,339

26. 6,254
    + 5,817
    12,071

27. 8,152
    + 1,369
    9,521

28. 8,674
    + 8,529
    17,203

29. 5,136
    + 3,278
    8,414

30. 8,769
    + 5,378
    14,147

31. 2,103
    + 8,936
    11,039

32. 8,966
    + 5,423
    14,389

Practice hard. You'll win.

Page 7

Addition

Name _____

Total Problems _____ 24
Problems Correct _____

1. 3,610
   + 2,874
   6,484

2. 8,317
   + 4,826
   13,143

3. 7,246
   + 8,395
   15,641

4. 6,380
   + 2,947
   9,327

5. 3,542
   + 4,879
   8,421

6. 8,700
   + 2,600
   11,300

7. 3,619
   + 2,845
   6,464

8. 4,725
   + 9,436
   14,161

9. 8,124
   + 6,397
   14,521

10. 6,314
    + 5,842
    12,156

11. 7,348
    + 5,476
    12,824

12. 3,018
    + 6,493
    9,511

13. 8,912
    + 3,869
    12,781

14. 3,264
    + 8,758
    12,022

15. 8,416
    + 5,657
    14,073

16. 8,712
    + 3,499
    12,211

17. 7,836
    + 4,379
    12,215

18. 2,468
    + 9,877
    12,345

19. 5,738
    + 5,684
    11,422

20. 3,648
    + 8,497
    12,145

21. 6,834
    + 7,496
    14,330

22. 2,695
    + 1,849
    4,544

23. 8,364
    + 3,987
    12,351

24. 9,285
    + 2,938
    12,223

Through practice you learn!

Page 8

Answer Key

Addition

Name _____

Total Problems ____26____

Problems Correct _____

1. 36 28 +41 **105**	2. 32 41 +25 **98**			
3. 43 66 +12 **121**	4. 26 82 +45 **153**	5. 26 34 +43 **103**	6. 63 76 +54 **193**	7. 24 75 +52 **151**
8. 53 26 +74 **153**	9. 34 16 +45 **95**	10. 42 34 +57 **133**	11. 621 354 +478 **1,453**	12. 429 362 +785 **1,576**
13. 537 629 +453 **1,619**	14. 648 832 +365 **1,845**	15. 724 568 +429 **1,721**	16. 853 467 +542 **1,862**	17. 542 863 +415 **1,820**
18. 853 276 +431 **1,560**	19. 514 372 +643 **1,529**	20. 254 126 +983 **1,363**	21. 2,657 1,389 +1,161 **5,207**	22. 8,162 1,113 +2,697 **11,972**
23. 3,432 3,671 +2,989 **10,092**	24. 6,387 1,212 +5,032 **12,631**	25. 1,291 2,799 +6,143 **10,233**	26. 8,792 1,733 +4,093 **14,618**	

Practice and anything's possible!

Addition

Name _____

Total Problems ____25____

Problems Correct _____

1. 12 15 89 +64 **180**	2. 47 34 86 +19 **186**			
3. 25 86 32 +27 **170**	4. 16 82 54 +93 **245**	5. 57 15 48 +26 **146**	6. 21 92 68 +91 **272**	7. 83 17 62 +95 **257**
8. 64 23 46 +69 **202**	9. 89 49 60 +24 **222**	10. 86 46 35 +24 **191**	11. 85 42 95 +26 **249**	12. 94 62 53 +48 **257**
13. 642 653 212 +324 **1,831**	14. 521 313 245 +686 **1,765**	15. 516 723 614 +932 **2,785**	16. 216 342 175 +129 **862**	17. 526 247 493 +312 **1,578**
18. 724 146 237 +413 **1,520**	19. 520 614 826 +439 **2,399**	20. 821 416 324 +515 **2,076**	21. 2,146 3,257 8,912 +1,674 **15,989**	22. 5,124 3,636 2,721 +1,419 **12,900**
23. 3,214 5,946 4,823 +2,152 **16,135**	24. 5,241 1,835 6,164 +5,496 **18,736**	25. 4,162 3,648 9,731 +1,229 **18,770**		

Practice brings success!

Addition

Name _____

Total Problems ____30____

Problems Correct _____

1. 52,618 +19,234 **71,852**	2. 83,614 +18,129 **101,743**			
3. 62,146 +29,373 **91,519**	4. 43,652 +28,934 **72,586**	5. 25,426 +63,817 **89,243**	6. 68,142 +71,528 **139,670**	7. 36,417 +28,528 **64,945**
8. 19,464 +36,925 **56,389**	9. 74,265 +19,548 **93,813**	10. 84,265 +92,381 **176,646**	11. 32,694 +89,213 **121,907**	12. 76,412 +89,258 **165,670**
13. 68,417 +47,528 **115,945**	14. 56,149 +38,273 **94,422**	15. 32,485 +86,291 **118,776**	16. 56,208 +92,489 **148,697**	17. 26,915 +64,823 **91,738**
18. 88,246 +34,193 **122,439**	19. 36,142 +31,233 **67,375**	20. 92,145 +28,362 **120,507**	21. 45,216 +29,843 **75,059**	22. 64,312 +89,248 **153,560**
23. 52,643 +89,342 **141,985**	24. 46,251 +57,484 **103,735**	25. 92,615 +63,218 **155,833**	26. 73,612 +21,429 **95,041**	27. 36,924 +52,385 **89,309**
28. 58,432 +91,251 **149,683**	29. 82,465 +19,328 **101,793**	30. 36,314 +82,808 **119,122**		

Practice makes perfect!

Subtraction

Name _____

Total Problems ____35____

Problems Correct _____

1. 3 -0 **3**	2. 6 -4 **2**	3. 2 -2 **0**				
4. 7 -2 **5**	5. 4 -4 **0**	6. 3 -3 **0**	7. 2 -1 **1**	8. 7 -3 **4**	9. 3 -1 **2**	10. 8 -2 **6**
11. 12 -3 **9**	12. 10 -2 **8**	13. 13 -4 **9**	14. 4 -3 **1**	15. 8 -4 **4**	16. 3 -2 **1**	17. 11 -3 **8**
18. 6 -3 **3**	19. 7 -4 **3**	20. 4 -2 **2**	21. 9 -4 **5**	22. 5 -3 **2**	23. 4 -1 **3**	24. 9 -2 **7**
25. 6 -2 **4**	26. 11 -4 **7**	27. 9 -3 **6**	28. 4 -0 **4**	29. 5 -2 **3**	30. 10 -3 **7**	31. 12 -4 **8**
32. 2 -0 **2**	33. 10 -4 **6**	34. 8 -3 **5**	35. 11 -2 **9**			

Practice brings success!

105

Answer Key

Subtraction

Skill: Subtraction of Digits 6-8

Name _____

Total Problems	36
Problems Correct	____

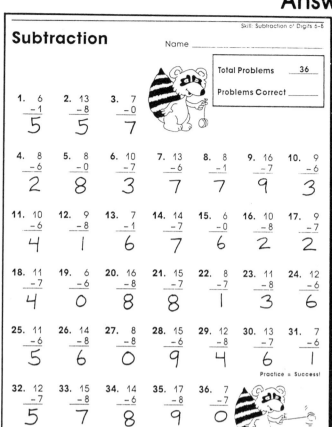

1. 6 − 1 = 5
2. 13 − 8 = 5
3. 7 − 0 = 7

4. 8 − 6 = 2
5. 8 − 0 = 8
6. 10 − 7 = 3
7. 13 − 6 = 7
8. 8 − 1 = 7
9. 16 − 7 = 9
10. 9 − 6 = 3

11. 10 − 6 = 4
12. 9 − 8 = 1
13. 7 − 1 = 6
14. 14 − 7 = 7
15. 6 − 0 = 6
16. 10 − 8 = 2
17. 9 − 7 = 2

18. 11 − 7 = 4
19. 6 − 6 = 0
20. 16 − 8 = 8
21. 15 − 7 = 8
22. 8 − 7 = 1
23. 11 − 8 = 3
24. 12 − 6 = 6

25. 11 − 6 = 5
26. 14 − 8 = 6
27. 8 − 8 = 0
28. 15 − 6 = 9
29. 12 − 8 = 4
30. 13 − 7 = 6
31. 7 − 6 = 1

Practice = Success!

32. 12 − 7 = 5
33. 15 − 8 = 7
34. 14 − 6 = 8
35. 17 − 8 = 9
36. 7 − 7 = 0

Page 13

Subtraction

Skill: Subtraction of Digits 7-9

Name _____

Total Problems	36
Problems Correct	____

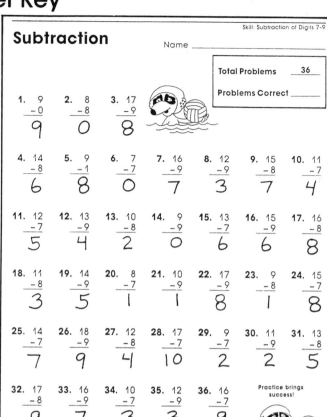

1. 9 − 0 = 9
2. 8 − 8 = 0
3. 17 − 9 = 8

4. 14 − 8 = 6
5. 9 − 1 = 8
6. 7 − 7 = 0
7. 16 − 9 = 7
8. 12 − 9 = 3
9. 15 − 8 = 7
10. 11 − 7 = 4

11. 12 − 7 = 5
12. 13 − 9 = 4
13. 10 − 8 = 2
14. 9 − 9 = 0
15. 13 − 7 = 6
16. 15 − 9 = 6
17. 16 − 8 = 8

18. 11 − 8 = 3
19. 14 − 9 = 5
20. 8 − 7 = 1
21. 10 − 9 = 1
22. 17 − 9 = 8
23. 9 − 8 = 1
24. 15 − 7 = 8

25. 14 − 7 = 7
26. 18 − 9 = 9
27. 12 − 8 = 4
28. 17 − 7 = 10
29. 9 − 7 = 2
30. 11 − 9 = 2
31. 13 − 8 = 5

Practice brings success!

32. 17 − 8 = 9
33. 16 − 9 = 7
34. 10 − 7 = 3
35. 12 − 9 = 3
36. 16 − 7 = 9

Page 14

Subtraction

Skill: Subtraction of Digits 1-9

Name _____

Total Problems	36
Problems Correct	____

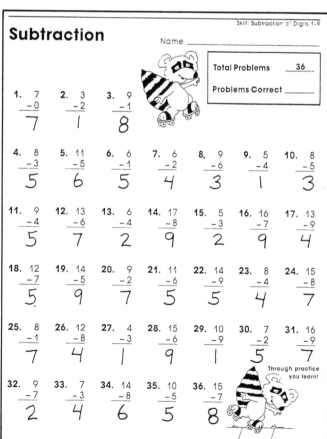

1. 7 − 0 = 7
2. 3 − 2 = 1
3. 9 − 1 = 8

4. 8 − 3 = 5
5. 11 − 5 = 6
6. 6 − 1 = 5
7. 6 − 2 = 4
8. 9 − 6 = 3
9. 5 − 4 = 1
10. 8 − 5 = 3

11. 9 − 4 = 5
12. 13 − 6 = 7
13. 6 − 4 = 2
14. 17 − 8 = 9
15. 5 − 3 = 2
16. 16 − 7 = 9
17. 13 − 9 = 4

18. 12 − 7 = 5
19. 14 − 5 = 9
20. 9 − 2 = 7
21. 11 − 6 = 5
22. 14 − 9 = 5
23. 8 − 4 = 4
24. 15 − 8 = 7

25. 8 − 1 = 7
26. 12 − 8 = 4
27. 4 − 3 = 1
28. 15 − 6 = 9
29. 10 − 9 = 1
30. 7 − 2 = 5
31. 16 − 9 = 7

Through practice you learn!

32. 9 − 7 = 2
33. 7 − 3 = 4
34. 14 − 8 = 6
35. 10 − 5 = 5
36. 15 − 7 = 8

Page 15

Subtraction

Skill: Two-Digit Subtraction-No Regrouping

Name _____

Total Problems	30
Problems Correct	____

1. 76 − 25 = 51
2. 49 − 24 = 25

3. 87 − 35 = 52
4. 75 − 52 = 23
5. 69 − 28 = 41
6. 43 − 31 = 12
7. 36 − 14 = 22

8. 93 − 51 = 42
9. 89 − 68 = 21
10. 37 − 22 = 15
11. 68 − 42 = 26
12. 59 − 33 = 26

13. 75 − 44 = 31
14. 65 − 31 = 34
15. 86 − 52 = 34
16. 39 − 13 = 26
17. 95 − 63 = 32

18. 61 − 30 = 31
19. 28 − 16 = 12
20. 98 − 76 = 22
21. 88 − 23 = 65
22. 73 − 22 = 51

23. 85 − 32 = 53
24. 78 − 42 = 36
25. 56 − 23 = 33
26. 94 − 61 = 33

Practice! Practice! Practice!

27. 82 − 31 = 51
28. 76 − 52 = 24
29. 85 − 74 = 11
30. 99 − 67 = 32

Page 16

Answer Key

Subtraction

Skill: Two-Digit Subtraction-Regrouping

Name _____

Total Problems ___30___

Problems Correct _____

1. 32
− 18
14

2. 64
− 38
26

3. 86
− 57
29

4. 70
− 28
42

5. 46
− 39
7

6. 54
− 26
28

7. 97
− 68
29

8. 80
− 73
7

9. 47
− 28
19

10. 76
− 59
17

11. 31
− 24
7

12. 52
− 35
17

13. 65
− 37
28

14. 42
− 27
15

15. 50
− 36
14

16. 73
− 46
27

17. 94
− 57
37

18. 72
− 49
23

19. 36
− 18
18

20. 85
− 27
58

21. 62
− 45
17

22. 28
− 19
9

23. 90
− 37
53

24. 57
− 28
29

25. 78
− 49
29

26. 64
− 45
19

Practice takes you to the top!

27. 86
− 38
48

28. 74
− 36
38

29. 91
− 74
17

30. 65
− 47
18

Page 17

Subtraction

Skill: Subtraction of Two- and Three-Digit Numbers

Name _____

Total Problems ___30___

Problems Correct _____

1. 64
− 29
35

2. 86
− 27
59

3. 58
− 29
29

4. 76
− 47
29

5. 35
− 18
17

6. 98
− 59
39

7. 76
− 68
8

8. 84
− 67
17

9. 48
− 39
9

10. 302
− 141
161

11. 624
− 251
373

12. 500
− 324
176

13. 432
− 341
91

14. 824
− 615
209

15. 735
− 382
353

16. 652
− 383
269

17. 927
− 463
464

18. 563
− 474
89

19. 327
− 149
178

20. 635
− 356
279

21. 723
− 248
475

22. 436
− 148
288

23. 867
− 279
588

24. 548
− 362
186

25. 724
− 537
187

26. 489
− 293
196

27. 954
− 567
387

28. 635
− 547
88

29. 840
− 382
458

30. 700
− 526
174

Practice and anything's possible!

Page 18

Subtraction

Skill: Three-Digit Subtraction-Regrouping

Name _____

Total Problems ___30___

Problems Correct _____

1. 500
− 247
253

2. 903
− 625
278

3. 720
− 384
336

4. 600
− 324
276

5. 800
− 423
377

6. 405
− 237
168

7. 707
− 418
289

8. 900
− 629
271

9. 508
− 269
239

10. 700
− 546
154

11. 300
− 173
127

12. 603
− 287
316

13. 807
− 358
449

14. 200
− 148
52

15. 900
− 356
544

16. 606
− 327
279

17. 700
− 268
432

18. 500
− 243
257

19. 805
− 527
278

20. 960
− 382
578

21. 307
− 198
109

22. 400
− 173
227

23. 200
− 154
46

24. 705
− 328
377

25. 502
− 236
266

26. 800
− 387
413

Practice = Success!

27. 900
− 629
271

28. 603
− 248
355

29. 708
− 539
169

30. 500
− 238
262

Page 19

Subtraction

Skill: Three-Digit Subtraction-Regrouping

Name _____

Total Problems ___30___

Problems Correct _____

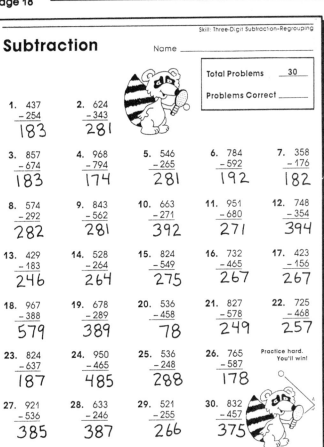

1. 437
− 254
183

2. 624
− 343
281

3. 857
− 674
183

4. 968
− 794
174

5. 546
− 265
281

6. 784
− 592
192

7. 358
− 176
182

8. 574
− 292
282

9. 843
− 562
281

10. 663
− 271
392

11. 951
− 680
271

12. 748
− 354
394

13. 429
− 183
246

14. 528
− 264
264

15. 824
− 549
275

16. 732
− 465
267

17. 423
− 156
267

18. 967
− 388
579

19. 678
− 289
389

20. 536
− 458
78

21. 827
− 578
249

22. 725
− 468
257

23. 824
− 637
187

24. 950
− 465
485

25. 536
− 248
288

26. 765
− 587
178

Practice hard. You'll win!

27. 921
− 536
385

28. 633
− 246
387

29. 521
− 255
266

30. 832
− 457
375

Page 20

Answer Key

Subtraction

Skill: Subtraction of Three- and Four-Digit Numbers

Name _____

Total Problems   30

Problems Correct _____

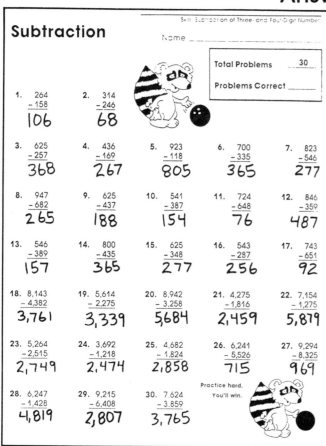

1. 264
   − 158
   106

2. 314
   − 246
   68

3. 625
   − 257
   368

4. 436
   − 169
   267

5. 923
   − 118
   805

6. 700
   − 335
   365

7. 823
   − 546
   277

8. 947
   − 682
   265

9. 625
   − 437
   188

10. 541
   − 387
   154

11. 724
   − 648
   76

12. 846
   − 359
   487

13. 546
   − 389
   157

14. 800
   − 435
   365

15. 625
   − 348
   277

16. 543
   − 287
   256

17. 743
   − 651
   92

18. 8,143
   − 4,382
   3,761

19. 5,614
   − 2,275
   3,339

20. 8,942
   − 3,258
   5,684

21. 4,275
   − 1,816
   2,459

22. 7,154
   − 1,275
   5,879

23. 5,264
   − 2,515
   2,749

24. 3,692
   − 1,218
   2,474

25. 4,682
   − 1,824
   2,858

26. 6,241
   − 5,526
   715

27. 9,294
   − 8,325
   969

28. 6,247
   − 1,428
   4,819

29. 9,215
   − 6,408
   2,807

30. 7,624
   − 3,859
   3,765

Practice hard.
You'll win.

Subtraction

Skill: Four-Digit Subtraction-Regrouping

Name _____

Total Problems   24

Problems Correct _____

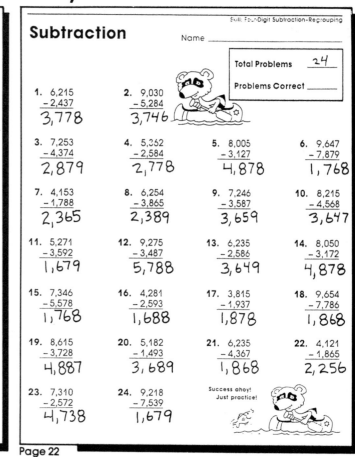

1. 6,215
   − 2,437
   3,778

2. 9,030
   − 5,284
   3,746

3. 7,253
   − 4,374
   2,879

4. 5,362
   − 2,584
   2,778

5. 8,005
   − 3,127
   4,878

6. 9,647
   − 7,879
   1,768

7. 4,153
   − 1,788
   2,365

8. 6,254
   − 3,865
   2,389

9. 7,246
   − 3,587
   3,659

10. 8,215
   − 4,568
   3,647

11. 5,271
   − 3,592
   1,679

12. 9,275
   − 3,487
   5,788

13. 6,235
   − 2,586
   3,649

14. 8,050
   − 3,172
   4,878

15. 7,346
   − 5,578
   1,768

16. 4,281
   − 2,593
   1,688

17. 3,815
   − 1,937
   1,878

18. 9,654
   − 7,786
   1,868

19. 8,615
   − 3,728
   4,887

20. 5,182
   − 1,493
   3,689

21. 6,235
   − 4,367
   1,868

22. 4,121
   − 1,865
   2,256

23. 7,310
   − 2,572
   4,738

24. 9,218
   − 7,539
   1,679

Success ahoy!
Just practice!

Subtraction

Skill: Subtraction of Four-Digit Numbers

Name _____

Total Problems   30

Problems Correct _____

1. 8,143
   − 2,532
   5,611

2. 5,146
   − 2,275
   2,871

3. 6,849
   − 4,723
   2,126

4. 9,243
   − 8,127
   1,116

5. 4,265
   − 2,193
   2,072

6. 8,546
   − 4,728
   3,818

7. 3,149
   − 2,027
   1,122

8. 5,267
   − 3,428
   1,839

9. 9,245
   − 5,863
   3,382

10. 7,648
   − 4,279
   3,369

11. 6,824
   − 4,372
   2,452

12. 8,765
   − 3,828
   4,937

13. 4,926
   − 2,357
   2,569

14. 8,643
   − 4,927
   3,716

15. 6,327
   − 5,138
   1,189

16. 3,864
   − 1,927
   1,937

17. 9,647
   − 6,478
   3,169

18. 7,524
   − 5,815
   1,709

19. 6,210
   − 4,128
   2,082

20. 8,247
   − 4,562
   3,685

21. 5,262
   − 3,534
   1,728

22. 4,893
   − 1,958
   2,935

23. 3,968
   − 1,279
   2,689

24. 8,259
   − 5,767
   2,492

25. 5,694
   − 3,836
   1,858

26. 9,265
   − 6,784
   2,481

27. 7,516
   − 3,427
   4,089

28. 6,800
   − 3,468
   3,332

29. 7,000
   − 2,632
   4,368

30. 9,214
   − 4,536
   4,678

Anything's possible
with practice!

Subtraction

Skill: Subtraction of Five-Digit Numbers

Name _____

Total Problems   30

Problems Correct _____

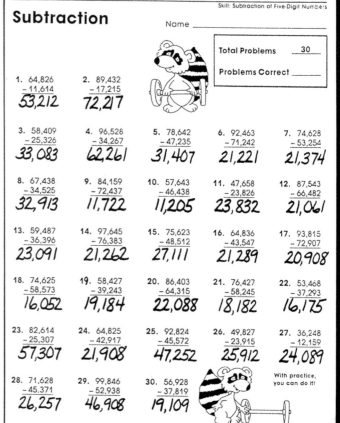

1. 64,826
   − 11,614
   53,212

2. 89,432
   − 17,215
   72,217

3. 58,409
   − 25,326
   33,083

4. 96,528
   − 34,267
   62,261

5. 78,642
   − 47,235
   31,407

6. 92,463
   − 71,242
   21,221

7. 74,628
   − 53,254
   21,374

8. 67,438
   − 34,525
   32,913

9. 84,159
   − 72,437
   11,722

10. 57,643
   − 46,438
   11,205

11. 47,658
   − 23,826
   23,832

12. 87,543
   − 66,482
   21,061

13. 59,487
   − 36,396
   23,091

14. 97,645
   − 76,383
   21,262

15. 75,623
   − 48,512
   27,111

16. 64,836
   − 43,547
   21,289

17. 93,815
   − 72,907
   20,908

18. 74,625
   − 58,573
   16,052

19. 58,427
   − 39,243
   19,184

20. 86,403
   − 64,315
   22,088

21. 76,427
   − 58,245
   18,182

22. 53,468
   − 37,293
   16,175

23. 82,614
   − 25,307
   57,307

24. 64,825
   − 42,917
   21,908

25. 92,824
   − 45,572
   47,252

26. 49,827
   − 23,915
   25,912

27. 36,248
   − 12,159
   24,089

28. 71,628
   − 45,371
   26,257

29. 99,846
   − 52,938
   46,908

30. 56,928
   − 37,819
   19,109

With practice,
you can do it!

Answer Key

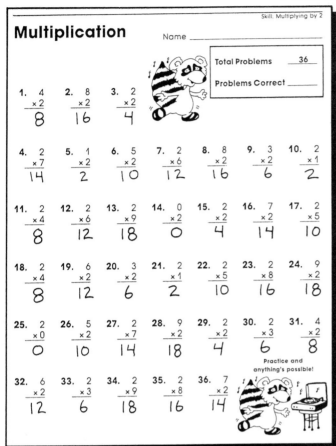

Skill: Multiplying by 2

Multiplication

Name _____

Total Problems ___36___

Problems Correct _____

1. 4 ×2 = **8**
2. 8 ×2 = **16**
3. 2 ×2 = **4**

4. 2 ×7 = **14**
5. 1 ×2 = **2**
6. 5 ×2 = **10**
7. 2 ×6 = **12**
8. 8 ×2 = **16**
9. 3 ×2 = **6**
10. 2 ×1 = **2**

11. 2 ×4 = **8**
12. 2 ×6 = **12**
13. 2 ×9 = **18**
14. 0 ×2 = **0**
15. 2 ×2 = **4**
16. 7 ×2 = **14**
17. 2 ×5 = **10**

18. 2 ×4 = **8**
19. 6 ×2 = **12**
20. 3 ×2 = **6**
21. 2 ×1 = **2**
22. 2 ×5 = **10**
23. 2 ×8 = **16**
24. 9 ×2 = **18**

25. 2 ×0 = **0**
26. 5 ×2 = **10**
27. 2 ×7 = **14**
28. 9 ×2 = **18**
29. 2 ×2 = **4**
30. 2 ×3 = **6**
31. 4 ×2 = **8**

Practice and anything's possible!

32. 6 ×2 = **12**
33. 2 ×3 = **6**
34. 2 ×9 = **18**
35. 2 ×8 = **16**
36. 7 ×2 = **14**

Page 25

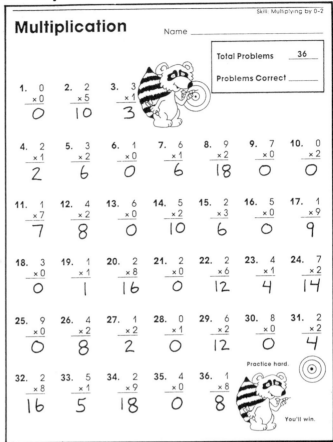

Skill: Multiplying by 0-2

Multiplication

Name _____

Total Problems ___36___

Problems Correct _____

1. 0 ×0 = **0**
2. 2 ×5 = **10**
3. 3 ×1 = **3**

4. 2 ×1 = **2**
5. 3 ×2 = **6**
6. 1 ×0 = **0**
7. 6 ×1 = **6**
8. 9 ×2 = **18**
9. 7 ×0 = **0**
10. 0 ×2 = **0**

11. 1 ×7 = **7**
12. 4 ×2 = **8**
13. 6 ×0 = **0**
14. 5 ×2 = **10**
15. 2 ×3 = **6**
16. 5 ×0 = **0**
17. 1 ×9 = **9**

18. 3 ×0 = **0**
19. 1 ×1 = **1**
20. 2 ×8 = **16**
21. 2 ×0 = **0**
22. 2 ×6 = **12**
23. 4 ×1 = **4**
24. 7 ×2 = **14**

25. 9 ×0 = **0**
26. 4 ×2 = **8**
27. 1 ×2 = **2**
28. 0 ×1 = **0**
29. 6 ×2 = **12**
30. 8 ×0 = **0**
31. 2 ×2 = **4**

Practice hard.

32. 2 ×8 = **16**
33. 5 ×1 = **5**
34. 2 ×9 = **18**
35. 4 ×0 = **0**
36. 1 ×8 = **8**

You'll win.

Page 26

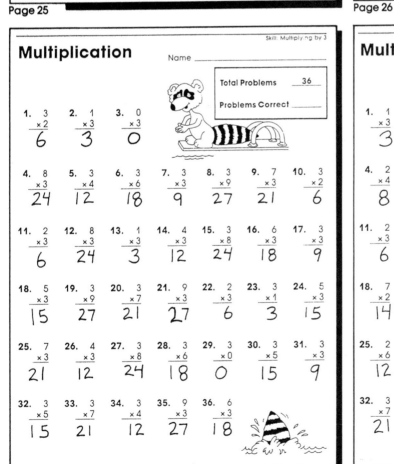

Skill: Multiplying by 3

Multiplication

Name _____

Total Problems ___36___

Problems Correct _____

1. 3 ×2 = **6**
2. 1 ×3 = **3**
3. 0 ×3 = **0**

4. 8 ×3 = **24**
5. 3 ×4 = **12**
6. 3 ×6 = **18**
7. 3 ×3 = **9**
8. 3 ×9 = **27**
9. 7 ×3 = **21**
10. 3 ×2 = **6**

11. 2 ×3 = **6**
12. 8 ×3 = **24**
13. 1 ×3 = **3**
14. 4 ×3 = **12**
15. 3 ×8 = **24**
16. 6 ×3 = **18**
17. 3 ×3 = **9**

18. 5 ×3 = **15**
19. 3 ×9 = **27**
20. 3 ×7 = **21**
21. 9 ×3 = **27**
22. 2 ×3 = **6**
23. 3 ×1 = **3**
24. 5 ×3 = **15**

25. 7 ×3 = **21**
26. 4 ×3 = **12**
27. 3 ×8 = **24**
28. 3 ×6 = **18**
29. 3 ×0 = **0**
30. 3 ×5 = **15**
31. 3 ×3 = **9**

32. 3 ×5 = **15**
33. 3 ×7 = **21**
34. 3 ×4 = **12**
35. 9 ×3 = **27**
36. 6 ×3 = **18**

Page 27

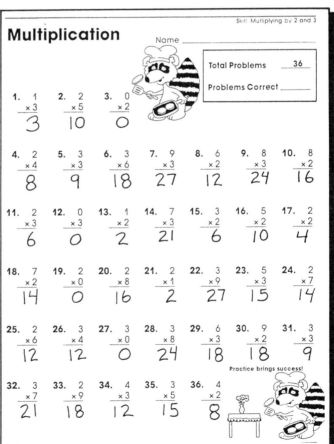

Skill: Multiplying by 2 and 3

Multiplication

Name _____

Total Problems ___36___

Problems Correct _____

1. 1 ×3 = **3**
2. 2 ×5 = **10**
3. 0 ×2 = **0**

4. 2 ×4 = **8**
5. 3 ×3 = **9**
6. 3 ×6 = **18**
7. 9 ×3 = **27**
8. 6 ×2 = **12**
9. 8 ×3 = **24**
10. 8 ×2 = **16**

11. 2 ×3 = **6**
12. 0 ×3 = **0**
13. 1 ×2 = **2**
14. 7 ×3 = **21**
15. 3 ×2 = **6**
16. 5 ×2 = **10**
17. 2 ×2 = **4**

18. 7 ×2 = **14**
19. 2 ×0 = **0**
20. 2 ×8 = **16**
21. 2 ×1 = **2**
22. 3 ×9 = **27**
23. 5 ×3 = **15**
24. 2 ×7 = **14**

25. 2 ×6 = **12**
26. 3 ×4 = **12**
27. 3 ×0 = **0**
28. 3 ×8 = **24**
29. 6 ×3 = **18**
30. 9 ×2 = **18**
31. 3 ×3 = **9**

Practice brings success!

32. 3 ×7 = **21**
33. 2 ×9 = **18**
34. 4 ×3 = **12**
35. 3 ×5 = **15**
36. 4 ×2 = **8**

Page 28

Answer Key

Multiplication

Name _____

Total Problems __35__

Problems Correct _____

1. 4 × 4 = 16
2. 0 × 4 = 0
3. 4 × 1 = 4
4. 4 × 2 = 8
5. 7 × 4 = 28
6. 6 × 4 = 24
7. 4 × 3 = 12
8. 9 × 4 = 36
9. 5 × 4 = 20
10. 4 × 8 = 32
11. 4 × 9 = 36
12. 1 × 4 = 4
13. 4 × 3 = 12
14. 4 × 7 = 28
15. 5 × 4 = 20
16. 4 × 4 = 16
17. 4 × 7 = 28
18. 4 × 4 = 16
19. 8 × 4 = 32
20. 2 × 4 = 8
21. 6 × 4 = 24
22. 4 × 0 = 0
23. 4 × 6 = 24
24. 3 × 4 = 12
25. 4 × 2 = 8
26. 4 × 8 = 32
27. 7 × 4 = 28
28. 4 × 5 = 20
29. 4 × 9 = 36
30. 8 × 4 = 32
31. 4 × 4 = 16
32. 9 × 4 = 36
33. 2 × 4 = 8
34. 4 × 6 = 24
35. 4 × 5 = 20

Practice = Success!

Page 29

Multiplication

Name _____

Total Problems __38__

Problems Correct _____

1. 12 × 3 = 36
2. 6 × 2 = 12
3. 3 × 5 = 15
4. 3 × 9 = 27
5. 4 × 4 = 16
6. 1 × 2 = 2
7. 4 × 12 = 48
8. 3 × 4 = 12
9. 11 × 2 = 22
10. 4 × 3 = 12
11. 2 × 3 = 6
12. 2 × 7 = 14
13. 2 × 4 = 8
14. 8 × 3 = 24
15. 10 × 4 = 40
16. 5 × 2 = 10
17. 12 × 4 = 48
18. 5 × 4 = 20
19. 2 × 2 = 4
20. 3 × 6 = 18
21. 11 × 3 = 33
22. 3 × 1 = 3
23. 4 × 9 = 36
24. 3 × 11 = 33
25. 10 × 2 = 20
26. 7 × 3 = 21
27. 8 × 4 = 32
28. 3 × 2 = 6
29. 1 × 4 = 4
30. 2 × 8 = 16
31. 7 × 4 = 28
32. 12 × 2 = 24
33. 6 × 4 = 24
34. 4 × 2 = 8
35. 11 × 4 = 44
36. 3 × 3 = 9
37. 2 × 9 = 18
38. 10 × 3 = 30

Practice makes perfect!

Page 30

Multiplication

Name _____

Total Problems __36__

Problems Correct _____

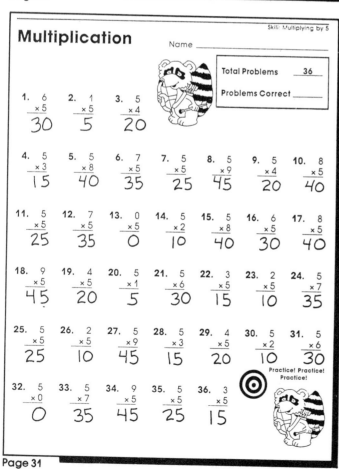

1. 6 × 5 = 30
2. 1 × 5 = 5
3. 5 × 4 = 20
4. 5 × 3 = 15
5. 5 × 8 = 40
6. 7 × 5 = 35
7. 5 × 5 = 25
8. 5 × 9 = 45
9. 5 × 4 = 20
10. 8 × 5 = 40
11. 5 × 5 = 25
12. 7 × 5 = 35
13. 0 × 5 = 0
14. 5 × 2 = 10
15. 5 × 8 = 40
16. 6 × 5 = 30
17. 8 × 5 = 40
18. 9 × 5 = 45
19. 4 × 5 = 20
20. 5 × 1 = 5
21. 5 × 6 = 30
22. 3 × 5 = 15
23. 2 × 5 = 10
24. 5 × 7 = 35
25. 5 × 5 = 25
26. 2 × 5 = 10
27. 5 × 9 = 45
28. 5 × 3 = 15
29. 4 × 5 = 20
30. 5 × 2 = 10
31. 5 × 6 = 30
32. 5 × 0 = 0
33. 5 × 7 = 35
34. 9 × 5 = 45
35. 5 × 5 = 25
36. 3 × 5 = 15

Practice! Practice! Practice!

Page 31

Multiplication

Name _____

Total Problems __36__

Problems Correct _____

1. 2 × 4 = 8
2. 4 × 4 = 16
3. 0 × 5 = 0
4. 4 × 6 = 24
5. 1 × 4 = 4
6. 8 × 5 = 40
7. 5 × 5 = 25
8. 8 × 4 = 32
9. 2 × 5 = 10
10. 4 × 5 = 20
11. 4 × 2 = 8
12. 5 × 2 = 10
13. 0 × 4 = 0
14. 7 × 5 = 35
15. 1 × 5 = 5
16. 5 × 4 = 20
17. 3 × 4 = 12
18. 7 × 4 = 28
19. 5 × 3 = 15
20. 4 × 2 = 8
21. 5 × 8 = 40
22. 9 × 4 = 36
23. 4 × 3 = 12
24. 5 × 5 = 25
25. 4 × 8 = 32
26. 4 × 1 = 4
27. 5 × 7 = 35
28. 3 × 5 = 15
29. 5 × 9 = 45
30. 6 × 4 = 24
31. 4 × 9 = 36
32. 9 × 5 = 45
33. 5 × 6 = 30
34. 5 × 3 = 15
35. 4 × 7 = 28
36. 6 × 5 = 30

Practice brings success!

Page 32

Answer Key

Multiplication — Page 33

Name _____

Total Problems __36__
Problems Correct _____

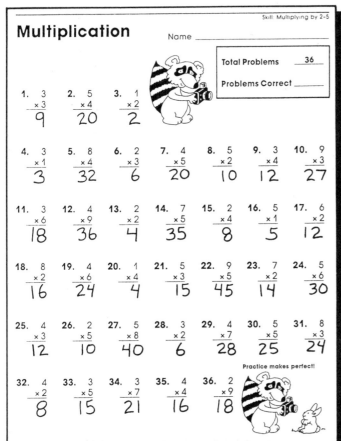

1. 3 ×3 = 9
2. 5 ×4 = 20
3. 1 ×2 = 2

4. 3 ×1 = 3
5. 8 ×4 = 32
6. 2 ×3 = 6
7. 4 ×5 = 20
8. 5 ×2 = 10
9. 3 ×4 = 12
10. 9 ×3 = 27

11. 3 ×6 = 18
12. 4 ×9 = 36
13. 2 ×2 = 4
14. 7 ×5 = 35
15. 2 ×4 = 8
16. 5 ×1 = 5
17. 6 ×2 = 12

18. 8 ×2 = 16
19. 4 ×6 = 24
20. 1 ×4 = 4
21. 5 ×3 = 15
22. 9 ×5 = 45
23. 7 ×2 = 14
24. 5 ×6 = 30

25. 4 ×3 = 12
26. 2 ×5 = 10
27. 5 ×8 = 40
28. 3 ×2 = 6
29. 4 ×7 = 28
30. 5 ×5 = 25
31. 8 ×3 = 24

32. 4 ×2 = 8
33. 3 ×5 = 15
34. 3 ×7 = 21
35. 4 ×4 = 16
36. 2 ×9 = 18

Practice makes perfect!

Page 33

Multiplication — Page 34

Name _____

Total Problems __36__
Problems Correct _____

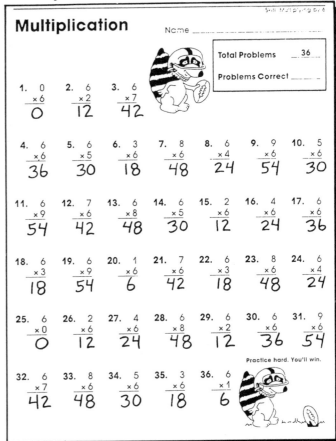

1. 0 ×6 = 0
2. 6 ×2 = 12
3. 6 ×7 = 42

4. 6 ×6 = 36
5. 6 ×5 = 30
6. 3 ×6 = 18
7. 8 ×6 = 48
8. 6 ×4 = 24
9. 9 ×6 = 54
10. 5 ×6 = 30

11. 6 ×9 = 54
12. 7 ×6 = 42
13. 6 ×8 = 48
14. 6 ×5 = 30
15. 2 ×6 = 12
16. 4 ×6 = 24
17. 6 ×6 = 36

18. 6 ×3 = 18
19. 6 ×9 = 54
20. 1 ×6 = 6
21. 7 ×6 = 42
22. 3 ×6 = 18
23. 8 ×6 = 48
24. 6 ×4 = 24

25. 6 ×0 = 0
26. 2 ×6 = 12
27. 4 ×6 = 24
28. 6 ×8 = 48
29. 6 ×2 = 12
30. 6 ×6 = 36
31. 9 ×6 = 54

32. 6 ×7 = 42
33. 8 ×6 = 48
34. 5 ×6 = 30
35. 3 ×6 = 18
36. 6 ×1 = 6

Practice hard. You'll win.

Page 34

Multiplication — Page 35

Name _____

Total Problems __36__
Problems Correct _____

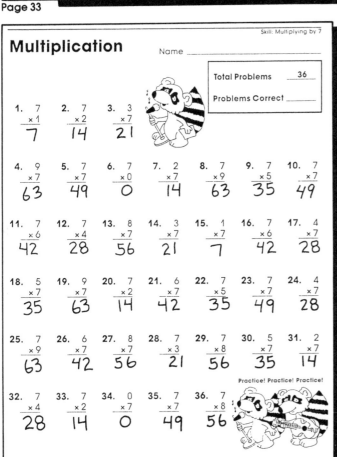

1. 7 ×1 = 7
2. 7 ×2 = 14
3. 3 ×7 = 21

4. 9 ×7 = 63
5. 7 ×7 = 49
6. 7 ×0 = 0
7. 2 ×7 = 14
8. 7 ×9 = 63
9. 7 ×5 = 35
10. 7 ×7 = 49

11. 7 ×6 = 42
12. 7 ×4 = 28
13. 8 ×7 = 56
14. 3 ×7 = 21
15. 1 ×7 = 7
16. 7 ×6 = 42
17. 4 ×7 = 28

18. 5 ×7 = 35
19. 9 ×7 = 63
20. 7 ×2 = 14
21. 6 ×7 = 42
22. 7 ×5 = 35
23. 7 ×7 = 49
24. 4 ×7 = 28

25. 7 ×9 = 63
26. 6 ×7 = 42
27. 8 ×7 = 56
28. 7 ×3 = 21
29. 7 ×8 = 56
30. 5 ×7 = 35
31. 2 ×7 = 14

32. 7 ×4 = 28
33. 7 ×2 = 14
34. 0 ×7 = 0
35. 7 ×7 = 49
36. 7 ×8 = 56

Practice! Practice! Practice!

Page 35

Multiplication — Page 36

Name _____

Total Problems __36__
Problems Correct _____

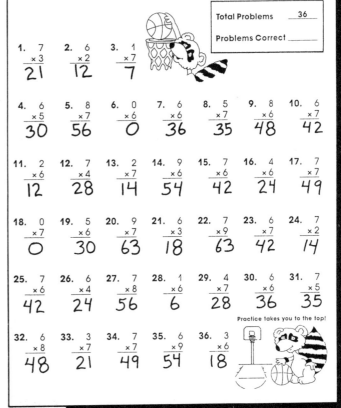

1. 7 ×3 = 21
2. 6 ×2 = 12
3. 1 ×7 = 7

4. 6 ×5 = 30
5. 8 ×7 = 56
6. 0 ×6 = 0
7. 6 ×6 = 36
8. 5 ×7 = 35
9. 8 ×6 = 48
10. 6 ×7 = 42

11. 2 ×6 = 12
12. 7 ×4 = 28
13. 2 ×7 = 14
14. 9 ×6 = 54
15. 7 ×6 = 42
16. 6 ×4 = 24
17. 7 ×7 = 49

18. 0 ×7 = 0
19. 5 ×6 = 30
20. 9 ×7 = 63
21. 6 ×3 = 18
22. 7 ×9 = 63
23. 6 ×7 = 42
24. 7 ×2 = 14

25. 7 ×6 = 42
26. 6 ×4 = 24
27. 7 ×8 = 56
28. 1 ×6 = 6
29. 4 ×7 = 28
30. 6 ×6 = 36
31. 7 ×5 = 35

32. 6 ×8 = 48
33. 3 ×7 = 21
34. 7 ×7 = 49
35. 6 ×9 = 54
36. 3 ×6 = 18

Practice takes you to the top!

Page 36

Answer Key

Multiplication

Name _____

Total Problems _____38_____

Problems Correct _____

1. 10 ×6 **60**	2. 2 ×5 **10**	3. 5 ×7 **35**

4. 7 ×5 **35**	5. 2 ×6 **12**	6. 7 ×7 **49**	7. 6 ×5 **30**	8. 11 ×7 **77**	9. 6 ×1 **6**	10. 12 ×5 **60**

| 11. 6 ×6 **36** | 12. 8 ×7 **56** | 13. 1 ×5 **5** | 14. 9 ×6 **54** | 15. 2 ×7 **14** | 16. 5 ×5 **25** | 17. 11 ×6 **66** |

| 18. 3 ×6 **18** | 19. 4 ×7 **28** | 20. 7 ×12 **84** | 21. 10 ×5 **50** | 22. 6 ×7 **42** | 23. 10 ×7 **70** | 24. 11 ×5 **55** |

| 25. 1 ×7 **7** | 26. 3 ×5 **15** | 27. 7 ×9 **63** | 28. 4 ×6 **24** | 29. 6 ×12 **72** | 30. 4 ×5 **20** | 31. 7 ×6 **42** |

| 32. 12 ×6 **72** | 33. 8 ×5 **40** | 34. 12 ×7 **84** | 35. 5 ×6 **30** |

Practice brings success!

| 36. 3 ×7 **21** | 37. 9 ×5 **45** | 38. 8 ×6 **48** |

Page 37

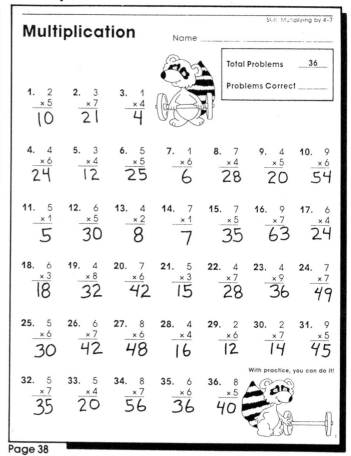

Multiplication

Name _____

Total Problems _____36_____

Problems Correct _____

1. 2 ×5 **10**	2. 3 ×7 **21**	3. 1 ×4 **4**

| 4. 4 ×6 **24** | 5. 3 ×4 **12** | 6. 5 ×5 **25** | 7. 1 ×6 **6** | 8. 7 ×4 **28** | 9. 4 ×5 **20** | 10. 9 ×6 **54** |

| 11. 5 ×1 **5** | 12. 6 ×5 **30** | 13. 4 ×2 **8** | 14. 7 ×1 **7** | 15. 7 ×5 **35** | 16. 9 ×7 **63** | 17. 6 ×4 **24** |

| 18. 6 ×3 **18** | 19. 4 ×8 **32** | 20. 7 ×6 **42** | 21. 5 ×3 **15** | 22. 4 ×7 **28** | 23. 4 ×9 **36** | 24. 7 ×7 **49** |

| 25. 5 ×6 **30** | 26. 6 ×7 **42** | 27. 8 ×6 **48** | 28. 4 ×4 **16** | 29. 2 ×6 **12** | 30. 2 ×7 **14** | 31. 9 ×5 **45** |

With practice, you can do it!

| 32. 5 ×7 **35** | 33. 5 ×4 **20** | 34. 8 ×7 **56** | 35. 6 ×6 **36** | 36. 8 ×5 **40** |

Page 38

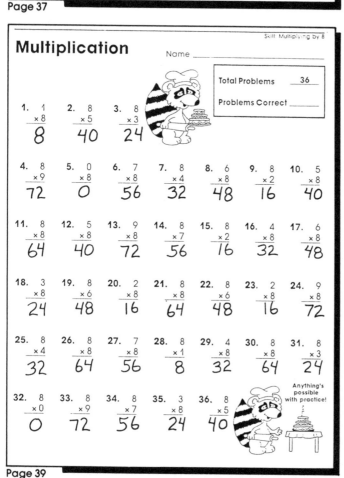

Multiplication

Name _____

Total Problems _____36_____

Problems Correct _____

1. 1 ×8 **8**	2. 8 ×5 **40**	3. 8 ×3 **24**

| 4. 8 ×9 **72** | 5. 0 ×8 **0** | 6. 7 ×8 **56** | 7. 8 ×4 **32** | 8. 6 ×8 **48** | 9. 8 ×2 **16** | 10. 5 ×8 **40** |

| 11. 8 ×8 **64** | 12. 5 ×8 **40** | 13. 9 ×8 **72** | 14. 8 ×7 **56** | 15. 8 ×2 **16** | 16. 4 ×8 **32** | 17. 6 ×8 **48** |

| 18. 3 ×8 **24** | 19. 8 ×6 **48** | 20. 2 ×8 **16** | 21. 8 ×8 **64** | 22. 8 ×6 **48** | 23. 2 ×8 **16** | 24. 9 ×8 **72** |

| 25. 8 ×4 **32** | 26. 8 ×8 **64** | 27. 7 ×8 **56** | 28. 8 ×1 **8** | 29. 4 ×8 **32** | 30. 8 ×8 **64** | 31. 8 ×3 **24** |

Anything's possible with practice!

| 32. 8 ×0 **0** | 33. 8 ×9 **72** | 34. 8 ×7 **56** | 35. 3 ×8 **24** | 36. 8 ×5 **40** |

Page 39

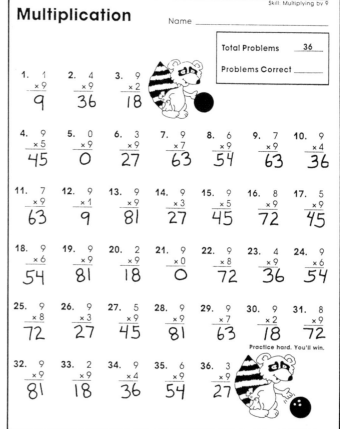

Multiplication

Name _____

Total Problems _____36_____

Problems Correct _____

1. 1 ×9 **9**	2. 4 ×9 **36**	3. 9 ×2 **18**

| 4. 9 ×5 **45** | 5. 0 ×9 **0** | 6. 3 ×9 **27** | 7. 9 ×7 **63** | 8. 6 ×9 **54** | 9. 7 ×9 **63** | 10. 9 ×4 **36** |

| 11. 7 ×9 **63** | 12. 9 ×1 **9** | 13. 9 ×9 **81** | 14. 9 ×3 **27** | 15. 9 ×5 **45** | 16. 8 ×9 **72** | 17. 5 ×9 **45** |

| 18. 9 ×6 **54** | 19. 9 ×9 **81** | 20. 2 ×9 **18** | 21. 9 ×0 **0** | 22. 9 ×8 **72** | 23. 4 ×9 **36** | 24. 9 ×6 **54** |

| 25. 9 ×8 **72** | 26. 9 ×3 **27** | 27. 5 ×9 **45** | 28. 9 ×9 **81** | 29. 9 ×7 **63** | 30. 9 ×2 **18** | 31. 8 ×9 **72** |

Practice hard. You'll win.

| 32. 9 ×9 **81** | 33. 2 ×9 **18** | 34. 9 ×4 **36** | 35. 6 ×9 **54** | 36. 3 ×9 **27** |

Page 40

Answer Key

Page 41

Multiplication

Name _____

Total Problems _____36_____

Problems Correct _____

1. 5 ×9 = 45
2. 2 ×8 = 16
3. 0 ×9 = 0

4. 9 ×8 = 72
5. 0 ×8 = 0
6. 9 ×4 = 36
7. 8 ×5 = 40
8. 9 ×2 = 18
9. 9 ×8 = 72
10. 9 ×9 = 81

11. 8 ×8 = 64
12. 2 ×9 = 18
13. 8 ×6 = 48
14. 9 ×5 = 45
15. 3 ×8 = 24
16. 1 ×9 = 9
17. 8 ×8 = 64

18. 4 ×8 = 32
19. 8 ×7 = 56
20. 6 ×9 = 54
21. 8 ×2 = 16
22. 8 ×9 = 72
23. 5 ×8 = 40
24. 9 ×6 = 54

25. 7 ×9 = 63
26. 8 ×3 = 24
27. 1 ×8 = 8
28. 3 ×9 = 27
29. 9 ×9 = 81
30. 7 ×8 = 56
31. 9 ×3 = 27

32. 8 ×9 = 72
33. 9 ×7 = 63
34. 4 ×9 = 36
35. 6 ×8 = 48
36. 8 ×4 = 32

Practice and anything's possible!

Page 41

Page 42

Multiplication

Name _____

Total Problems _____36_____

Problems Correct _____

1. 8 ×2 = 16
2. 4 ×6 = 24
3. 7 ×1 = 7

4. 9 ×6 = 54
5. 8 ×8 = 64
6. 7 ×5 = 35
7. 1 ×6 = 6
8. 8 ×7 = 56
9. 8 ×6 = 48
10. 7 ×9 = 63

11. 7 ×4 = 28
12. 1 ×8 = 8
13. 7 ×8 = 56
14. 6 ×2 = 12
15. 8 ×5 = 40
16. 9 ×1 = 9
17. 7 ×6 = 42

18. 3 ×6 = 18
19. 6 ×8 = 48
20. 2 ×7 = 14
21. 6 ×9 = 54
22. 7 ×7 = 49
23. 8 ×9 = 72
24. 9 ×3 = 27

25. 6 ×7 = 42
26. 9 ×9 = 81
27. 3 ×8 = 24
28. 5 ×9 = 45
29. 5 ×6 = 30
30. 2 ×9 = 18
31. 9 ×8 = 72

32. 9 ×7 = 63
33. 4 ×9 = 36
34. 6 ×6 = 36
35. 4 ×8 = 32
36. 3 ×7 = 21

Practice makes perfect!

Page 42

Page 43

Multiplication

Name _____

Total Problems _____36_____

Problems Correct _____

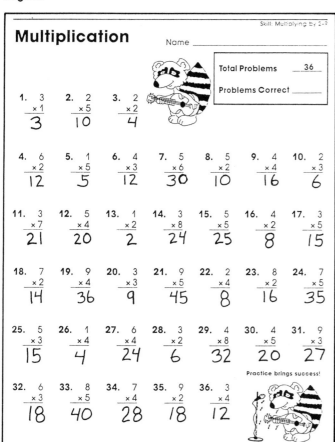

1. 3 ×1 = 3
2. 2 ×5 = 10
3. 2 ×2 = 4

4. 6 ×2 = 12
5. 1 ×5 = 5
6. 4 ×3 = 12
7. 5 ×6 = 30
8. 5 ×2 = 10
9. 4 ×4 = 16
10. 2 ×3 = 6

11. 3 ×7 = 21
12. 5 ×4 = 20
13. 1 ×2 = 2
14. 3 ×8 = 24
15. 5 ×5 = 25
16. 4 ×2 = 8
17. 3 ×5 = 15

18. 7 ×2 = 14
19. 9 ×4 = 36
20. 3 ×3 = 9
21. 9 ×5 = 45
22. 2 ×4 = 8
23. 8 ×2 = 16
24. 7 ×5 = 35

25. 5 ×3 = 15
26. 1 ×4 = 4
27. 6 ×4 = 24
28. 3 ×2 = 6
29. 4 ×8 = 32
30. 4 ×5 = 20
31. 9 ×3 = 27

32. 6 ×3 = 18
33. 8 ×5 = 40
34. 7 ×4 = 28
35. 9 ×2 = 18
36. 3 ×4 = 12

Practice brings success!

Page 43

Page 44

Multiplication

Name _____

Total Problems _____36_____

Problems Correct _____

1. 0 ×7 = 0
2. 4 ×3 = 12
3. 1 ×5 = 5

4. 4 ×8 = 32
5. 3 ×6 = 18
6. 5 ×5 = 25
7. 9 ×6 = 54
8. 4 ×2 = 8
9. 2 ×6 = 12
10. 4 ×7 = 28

11. 2 ×5 = 10
12. 6 ×6 = 36
13. 1 ×4 = 4
14. 4 ×5 = 20
15. 8 ×6 = 48
16. 4 ×9 = 36
17. 5 ×6 = 30

18. 6 ×5 = 30
19. 7 ×3 = 21
20. 4 ×4 = 16
21. 4 ×6 = 24
22. 7 ×9 = 63
23. 7 ×5 = 35
24. 7 ×7 = 49

25. 7 ×4 = 28
26. 5 ×9 = 45
27. 0 ×6 = 0
28. 3 ×5 = 15
29. 5 ×7 = 35
30. 6 ×4 = 24
31. 6 ×7 = 42

32. 8 ×5 = 40
33. 2 ×7 = 14
34. 8 ×7 = 56
35. 5 ×4 = 20
36. 7 ×6 = 42

Practice and anything's possible!

Page 44

Answer Key

Multiplication

Name _____

Total Problems __36__

Problems Correct _____

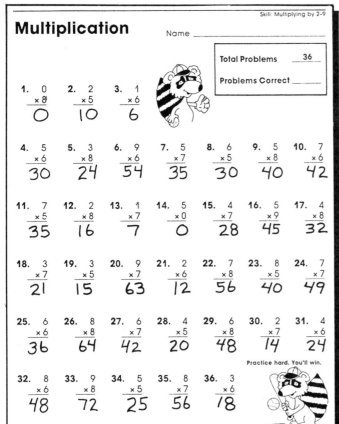

1. 0 ×8 = 0
2. 2 ×5 = 10
3. 1 ×6 = 6
4. 5 ×6 = 30
5. 3 ×8 = 24
6. 9 ×6 = 54
7. 5 ×7 = 35
8. 6 ×5 = 30
9. 5 ×8 = 40
10. 7 ×6 = 42
11. 7 ×5 = 35
12. 2 ×8 = 16
13. 1 ×7 = 7
14. 5 ×0 = 0
15. 4 ×7 = 28
16. 5 ×9 = 45
17. 4 ×8 = 32
18. 3 ×7 = 21
19. 3 ×5 = 15
20. 9 ×7 = 63
21. 2 ×6 = 12
22. 7 ×8 = 56
23. 8 ×5 = 40
24. 7 ×7 = 49
25. 6 ×6 = 36
26. 8 ×8 = 64
27. 6 ×7 = 42
28. 4 ×5 = 20
29. 6 ×8 = 48
30. 2 ×7 = 14
31. 4 ×6 = 24
32. 8 ×6 = 48
33. 9 ×8 = 72
34. 5 ×5 = 25
35. 8 ×7 = 56
36. 3 ×6 = 18

Practice hard. You'll win.

Page 45

Multiplication

Name _____

Total Problems __36__

Problems Correct _____

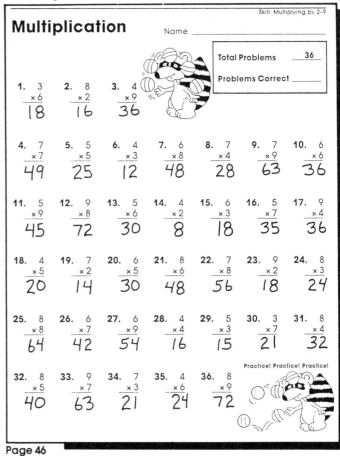

1. 3 ×6 = 18
2. 8 ×2 = 16
3. 4 ×9 = 36
4. 7 ×7 = 49
5. 5 ×5 = 25
6. 4 ×3 = 12
7. 6 ×8 = 48
8. 7 ×4 = 28
9. 7 ×9 = 63
10. 6 ×6 = 36
11. 5 ×9 = 45
12. 9 ×8 = 72
13. 5 ×6 = 30
14. 4 ×2 = 8
15. 6 ×3 = 18
16. 5 ×7 = 35
17. 9 ×4 = 36
18. 4 ×5 = 20
19. 7 ×2 = 14
20. 6 ×5 = 30
21. 8 ×6 = 48
22. 7 ×8 = 56
23. 9 ×2 = 18
24. 8 ×3 = 24
25. 8 ×8 = 64
26. 6 ×7 = 42
27. 6 ×9 = 54
28. 4 ×4 = 16
29. 5 ×3 = 15
30. 3 ×7 = 21
31. 8 ×4 = 32
32. 8 ×5 = 40
33. 9 ×7 = 63
34. 7 ×3 = 21
35. 4 ×6 = 24
36. 8 ×9 = 72

Practice! Practice! Practice!

Page 46

Multiplication

Name _____

Total Problems __38__

Problems Correct _____

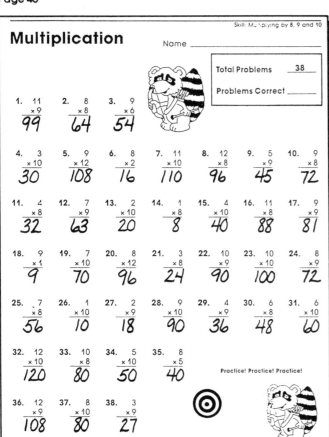

1. 11 ×9 = 99
2. 8 ×8 = 64
3. 9 ×6 = 54
4. 3 ×10 = 30
5. 9 ×12 = 108
6. 8 ×2 = 16
7. 11 ×10 = 110
8. 12 ×8 = 96
9. 5 ×9 = 45
10. 9 ×8 = 72
11. 4 ×8 = 32
12. 7 ×9 = 63
13. 2 ×10 = 20
14. 1 ×8 = 8
15. 4 ×10 = 40
16. 11 ×8 = 88
17. 9 ×9 = 81
18. 9 ×1 = 9
19. 7 ×10 = 70
20. 8 ×12 = 96
21. 3 ×8 = 24
22. 10 ×9 = 90
23. 10 ×10 = 100
24. 8 ×9 = 72
25. 7 ×8 = 56
26. 1 ×10 = 10
27. 2 ×9 = 18
28. 9 ×10 = 90
29. 4 ×9 = 36
30. 6 ×8 = 48
31. 6 ×10 = 60
32. 12 ×10 = 120
33. 10 ×8 = 80
34. 5 ×10 = 50
35. 8 ×5 = 40
36. 12 ×9 = 108
37. 8 ×10 = 80
38. 3 ×9 = 27

Practice! Practice! Practice!

Page 47

Multiplication

Name _____

Total Problems __38__

Problems Correct _____

1. 11 ×6 = 66
2. 1 ×11 = 11
3. 5 ×12 = 60
4. 7 ×11 = 77
5. 12 ×11 = 132
6. 12 ×12 = 144
7. 4 ×12 = 48
8. 6 ×11 = 66
9. 11 ×12 = 132
10. 11 ×11 = 121
11. 5 ×11 = 55
12. 11 ×7 = 77
13. 6 ×12 = 72
14. 12 ×9 = 108
15. 10 ×11 = 110
16. 10 ×12 = 120
17. 12 ×8 = 96
18. 3 ×12 = 36
19. 11 ×9 = 99
20. 2 ×11 = 22
21. 9 ×12 = 108
22. 12 ×7 = 84
23. 11 ×4 = 44
24. 2 ×12 = 24
25. 12 ×12 = 144
26. 1 ×12 = 12
27. 11 ×10 = 110
28. 9 ×11 = 99
29. 12 ×11 = 132
30. 8 ×12 = 96
31. 11 ×9 = 99
32. 11 ×8 = 88
33. 12 ×10 = 120
34. 3 ×11 = 33
35. 7 ×12 = 84
36. 12 ×6 = 72
37. 8 ×11 = 88
38. 12 ×1 = 12

Practice = Success!

Page 48

Answer Key

Multiplication

Name _____

Total Problems __30__

Problems Correct _____

1. 32 × 3 = 96
2. 21 × 4 = 84
3. 43 × 2 = 86
4. 20 × 3 = 60
5. 11 × 4 = 44
6. 34 × 2 = 68
7. 21 × 3 = 63
8. 33 × 3 = 99
9. 24 × 2 = 48
10. 22 × 4 = 88
11. 40 × 2 = 80
12. 32 × 2 = 64
13. 13 × 3 = 39
14. 22 × 2 = 44
15. 20 × 4 = 80
16. 23 × 2 = 46
17. 11 × 3 = 33
18. 41 × 2 = 82
19. 31 × 3 = 93
20. 44 × 2 = 88
21. 23 × 3 = 69
22. 12 × 4 = 48
23. 33 × 2 = 66
24. 30 × 3 = 90
25. 21 × 2 = 42
26. 13 × 2 = 26
27. 42 × 2 = 84
28. 12 × 3 = 36
29. 14 × 2 = 28
30. 22 × 3 = 66

Practice makes perfect!

Page 49

Multiplication

Name _____

Total Problems __30__

Problems Correct _____

1. 26 × 3 = 78
2. 24 × 4 = 96
3. 39 × 2 = 78
4. 14 × 7 = 98
5. 25 × 3 = 75
6. 13 × 5 = 65
7. 37 × 2 = 74
8. 48 × 2 = 96
9. 23 × 4 = 92
10. 35 × 2 = 70
11. 12 × 8 = 96
12. 24 × 3 = 72
13. 13 × 6 = 78
14. 18 × 5 = 90
15. 29 × 3 = 87
16. 17 × 5 = 85
17. 49 × 2 = 98
18. 16 × 6 = 96
19. 36 × 2 = 72
20. 18 × 3 = 54
21. 15 × 6 = 90
22. 27 × 3 = 81
23. 13 × 7 = 91
24. 28 × 3 = 84
25. 19 × 5 = 95
26. 46 × 2 = 92
27. 16 × 5 = 80
28. 47 × 2 = 94
29. 14 × 6 = 84
30. 53 × 4 = 212

With practice, you can do it!

Page 50

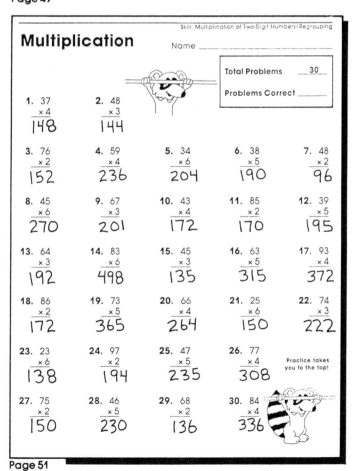

Multiplication

Name _____

Total Problems __30__

Problems Correct _____

1. 37 × 4 = 148
2. 48 × 3 = 144
3. 76 × 2 = 152
4. 59 × 4 = 236
5. 34 × 6 = 204
6. 38 × 5 = 190
7. 48 × 2 = 96
8. 45 × 6 = 270
9. 67 × 3 = 201
10. 43 × 4 = 172
11. 85 × 2 = 170
12. 39 × 5 = 195
13. 64 × 3 = 192
14. 83 × 6 = 498
15. 45 × 3 = 135
16. 63 × 5 = 315
17. 93 × 4 = 372
18. 86 × 2 = 172
19. 73 × 5 = 365
20. 66 × 4 = 264
21. 25 × 6 = 150
22. 74 × 3 = 222
23. 23 × 6 = 138
24. 97 × 2 = 194
25. 47 × 5 = 235
26. 77 × 4 = 308
27. 75 × 2 = 150
28. 46 × 5 = 230
29. 68 × 2 = 136
30. 84 × 4 = 336

Practice takes you to the top!

Page 51

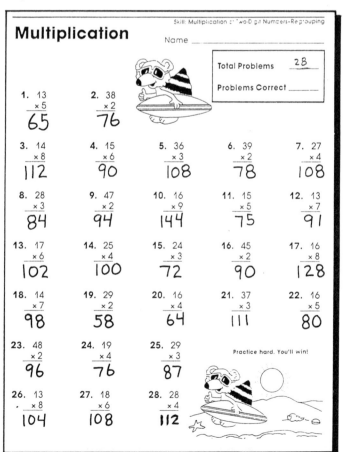

Multiplication

Name _____

Total Problems __28__

Problems Correct _____

1. 13 × 5 = 65
2. 38 × 2 = 76
3. 14 × 8 = 112
4. 15 × 6 = 90
5. 36 × 3 = 108
6. 39 × 2 = 78
7. 27 × 4 = 108
8. 28 × 3 = 84
9. 47 × 2 = 94
10. 16 × 9 = 144
11. 15 × 5 = 75
12. 13 × 7 = 91
13. 17 × 6 = 102
14. 25 × 4 = 100
15. 24 × 3 = 72
16. 45 × 2 = 90
17. 16 × 8 = 128
18. 14 × 7 = 98
19. 29 × 2 = 58
20. 16 × 4 = 64
21. 37 × 3 = 111
22. 16 × 5 = 80
23. 48 × 2 = 96
24. 19 × 4 = 76
25. 29 × 3 = 87
26. 13 × 8 = 104
27. 18 × 6 = 108
28. 28 × 4 = 112

Practice hard. You'll win!

Page 52

Answer Key

Multiplication

Name _____

Total Problems ___30___

Problems Correct _____

1. 26
   ×3
   78

2. 64
   ×5
   320

3. 43
   ×8
   344

4. 57
   ×6
   342

5. 98
   ×2
   196

6. 35
   ×4
   140

7. 76
   ×3
   228

8. 46
   ×7
   322

9. 85
   ×3
   255

10. 35
   ×8
   280

11. 23
   ×9
   207

12. 62
   ×5
   310

13. 42
   ×6
   252

14. 73
   ×4
   292

15. 82
   ×5
   410

16. 67
   ×3
   201

17. 27
   ×8
   216

18. 49
   ×7
   343

19. 88
   ×2
   176

20. 36
   ×9
   324

21. 53
   ×6
   318

22. 83
   ×4
   332

23. 65
   ×5
   325

24. 34
   ×8
   272

25. 47
   ×6
   282

26. 28
   ×3
   84

27. 34
   ×7
   238

Practice brings success!

28. 83
   ×4
   332

29. 35
   ×6
   210

30. 73
   ×8
   584

Page 53

Multiplication

Name _____

Total Problems ___30___

Problems Correct _____

1. 84
   ×5
   420

2. 35
   ×7
   245

3. 63
   ×8
   504

4. 57
   ×4
   228

5. 55
   ×9
   495

6. 43
   ×6
   258

7. 92
   ×8
   736

8. 42
   ×9
   378

9. 85
   ×6
   510

10. 53
   ×4
   212

11. 74
   ×8
   592

12. 83
   ×5
   415

13. 65
   ×7
   455

14. 87
   ×3
   261

15. 49
   ×6
   294

16. 23
   ×9
   207

17. 86
   ×4
   344

18. 35
   ×8
   280

19. 82
   ×5
   410

20. 32
   ×9
   288

21. 46
   ×6
   276

22. 89
   ×2
   178

With practice,
you can do it!

23. 64
   ×7
   448

24. 43
   ×9
   387

25. 28
   ×6
   168

26. 59
   ×8
   472

27. 72
   ×5
   360

28. 44
   ×9
   396

29. 84
   ×7
   588

30. 53
   ×6
   318

Page 54

Multiplication

Name _____

Total Problems ___30___

Problems Correct _____

1. 76
   ×4
   304

2. 23
   ×6
   138

3. 49
   ×8
   392

4. 64
   ×5
   320

5. 87
   ×9
   783

6. 43
   ×7
   301

7. 88
   ×3
   264

8. 73
   ×6
   438

9. 54
   ×8
   432

10. 69
   ×5
   345

11. 74
   ×9
   666

12. 39
   ×7
   273

13. 83
   ×9
   747

14. 45
   ×6
   270

15. 75
   ×8
   600

16. 62
   ×7
   434

17. 28
   ×9
   252

18. 52
   ×8
   416

19. 63
   ×5
   315

20. 77
   ×3
   231

21. 38
   ×9
   342

22. 97
   ×2
   194

23. 48
   ×7
   336

24. 53
   ×9
   477

25. 29
   ×7
   203

26. 37
   ×8
   296

Practice puts
you on top!

27. 57
   ×6
   342

28. 48
   ×8
   384

29. 73
   ×9
   657

30. 82
   ×7
   574

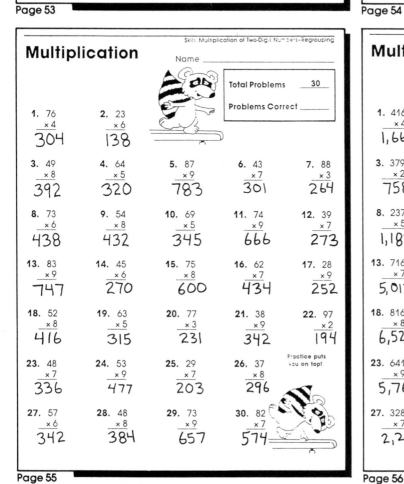

Page 55

Multiplication

Name _____

Total Problems ___30___

Problems Correct _____

1. 416
   ×4
   1,664

2. 318
   ×6
   1,908

3. 379
   ×2
   758

4. 719
   ×9
   6,471

5. 168
   ×7
   1,176

6. 713
   ×8
   5,704

7. 219
   ×6
   1,314

8. 237
   ×5
   1,185

9. 279
   ×3
   837

10. 173
   ×9
   1,557

11. 164
   ×6
   984

12. 179
   ×8
   1,432

13. 716
   ×7
   5,012

14. 298
   ×4
   1,192

15. 836
   ×3
   2,508

16. 632
   ×5
   3,160

17. 218
   ×9
   1,962

18. 816
   ×8
   6,528

19. 421
   ×6
   2,526

20. 248
   ×2
   496

21. 541
   ×7
   3,787

22. 918
   ×4
   3,672

23. 641
   ×9
   5,769

24. 836
   ×3
   2,508

25. 941
   ×8
   7,528

26. 917
   ×6
   5,502

Practice
puts you on top!

27. 328
   ×7
   2,296

28. 812
   ×9
   7,308

29. 621
   ×7
   4,347

30. 713
   ×8
   5,704

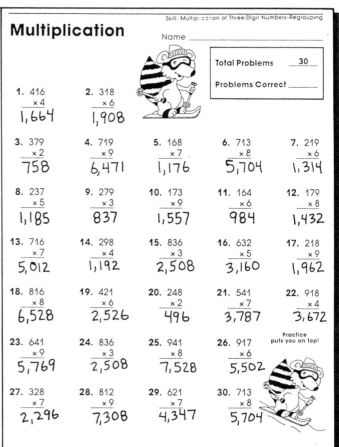

Page 56

Answer Key

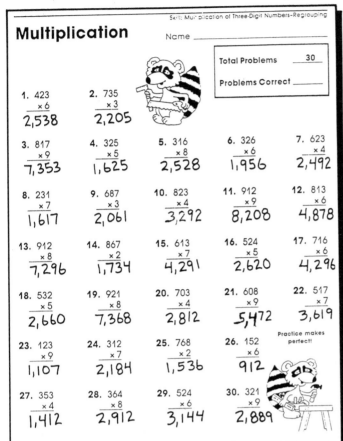

Multiplication

Name _____

Skill: Multiplication of Three-Digit Numbers–Regrouping

Total Problems ___30___

Problems Correct _____

1. 423 ×6 = 2,538	2. 735 ×3 = 2,205			
3. 817 ×9 = 7,353	4. 325 ×5 = 1,625	5. 316 ×8 = 2,528	6. 326 ×6 = 1,956	7. 623 ×4 = 2,492
8. 231 ×7 = 1,617	9. 687 ×3 = 2,061	10. 823 ×4 = 3,292	11. 912 ×9 = 8,208	12. 813 ×6 = 4,878
13. 912 ×8 = 7,296	14. 867 ×2 = 1,734	15. 613 ×7 = 4,291	16. 524 ×5 = 2,620	17. 716 ×6 = 4,296
18. 532 ×5 = 2,660	19. 921 ×8 = 7,368	20. 703 ×4 = 2,812	21. 608 ×9 = 5,472	22. 517 ×7 = 3,619
23. 123 ×9 = 1,107	24. 312 ×7 = 2,184	25. 768 ×2 = 1,536	26. 152 ×6 = 912	Practice makes perfect!
27. 353 ×4 = 1,412	28. 364 ×8 = 2,912	29. 524 ×6 = 3,144	30. 321 ×9 = 2,889	

Page 57

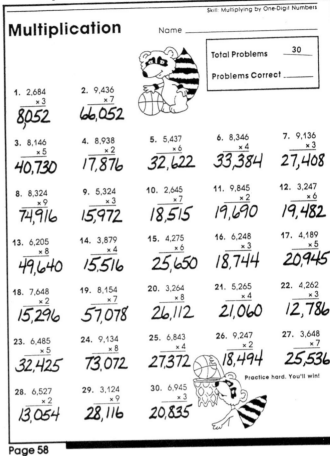

Multiplication

Name _____

Skill: Multiplying by One-Digit Numbers

Total Problems ___30___

Problems Correct _____

1. 2,684 ×3 = 8,052	2. 9,436 ×7 = 66,052			
3. 8,146 ×5 = 40,730	4. 8,938 ×2 = 17,876	5. 5,437 ×6 = 32,622	6. 8,346 ×4 = 33,384	7. 9,136 ×3 = 27,408
8. 8,324 ×9 = 74,916	9. 5,324 ×3 = 15,972	10. 2,645 ×7 = 18,515	11. 9,845 ×2 = 19,690	12. 3,247 ×6 = 19,482
13. 6,205 ×8 = 49,640	14. 3,879 ×4 = 15,516	15. 4,275 ×6 = 25,650	16. 6,248 ×3 = 18,744	17. 4,189 ×5 = 20,945
18. 7,648 ×2 = 15,296	19. 8,154 ×7 = 57,078	20. 3,264 ×8 = 26,112	21. 5,265 ×4 = 21,060	22. 4,262 ×3 = 12,786
23. 6,485 ×5 = 32,425	24. 9,134 ×8 = 73,072	25. 6,843 ×4 = 27,372	26. 9,247 ×2 = 18,494	27. 3,648 ×7 = 25,536
28. 6,527 ×2 = 13,054	29. 3,124 ×9 = 28,116	30. 6,945 ×3 = 20,835	Practice hard. You'll win!	

Page 58

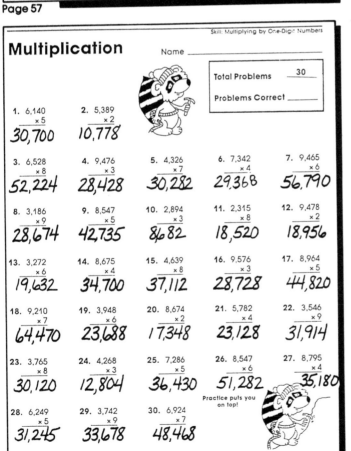

Multiplication

Name _____

Skill: Multiplying by One-Digit Numbers

Total Problems ___30___

Problems Correct _____

1. 6,140 ×5 = 30,700	2. 5,389 ×2 = 10,778			
3. 6,528 ×8 = 52,224	4. 9,476 ×3 = 28,428	5. 4,326 ×7 = 30,282	6. 7,342 ×4 = 29,368	7. 9,465 ×6 = 56,790
8. 3,186 ×9 = 28,674	9. 8,547 ×5 = 42,735	10. 2,894 ×3 = 8,682	11. 2,315 ×8 = 18,520	12. 9,478 ×2 = 18,956
13. 3,272 ×6 = 19,632	14. 8,675 ×4 = 34,700	15. 4,639 ×8 = 37,112	16. 9,576 ×3 = 28,728	17. 8,964 ×5 = 44,820
18. 9,210 ×7 = 64,470	19. 3,948 ×6 = 23,688	20. 8,674 ×2 = 17,348	21. 5,782 ×4 = 23,128	22. 3,546 ×9 = 31,914
23. 3,765 ×8 = 30,120	24. 4,268 ×3 = 12,804	25. 7,286 ×5 = 36,430	26. 8,547 ×6 = 51,282	27. 8,795 ×4 = 35,180
28. 6,249 ×5 = 31,245	29. 3,742 ×9 = 33,678	30. 6,924 ×7 = 48,468	Practice puts you on top!	

Page 59

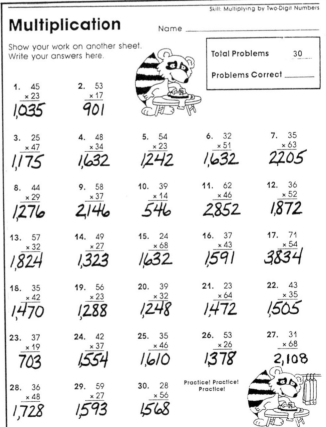

Multiplication

Name _____

Skill: Multiplying by Two-Digit Numbers

Show your work on another sheet.
Write your answers here.

Total Problems ___30___

Problems Correct _____

1. 45 ×23 = 1,035	2. 53 ×17 = 901			
3. 25 ×47 = 1,175	4. 48 ×34 = 1,632	5. 54 ×23 = 1242	6. 32 ×51 = 1,632	7. 35 ×63 = 2205
8. 44 ×29 = 1276	9. 58 ×37 = 2,146	10. 39 ×14 = 546	11. 62 ×46 = 2,852	12. 36 ×52 = 1,872
13. 57 ×32 = 1,824	14. 49 ×27 = 1,323	15. 24 ×68 = 1,632	16. 37 ×43 = 1,591	17. 71 ×54 = 3,834
18. 35 ×42 = 1,470	19. 56 ×23 = 1,288	20. 39 ×32 = 1,248	21. 23 ×64 = 1,472	22. 43 ×35 = 1,505
23. 37 ×19 = 703	24. 42 ×37 = 1,554	25. 35 ×46 = 1,610	26. 53 ×26 = 1,378	27. 31 ×68 = 2,108
28. 36 ×48 = 1,728	29. 59 ×27 = 1,593	30. 28 ×56 = 1,568	Practice! Practice! Practice!	

Page 60

Math IF8740

117

© 1990 Instructional Fair, Inc.

Answer Key

Multiplication

Skill: Multiplying by Two-Digit Numbers

Name _____

Show your work on another sheet.
Write your answers here.

Total Problems __30__

Problems Correct _____

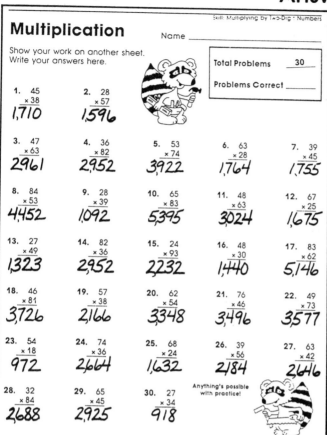

1. 45 × 38 = 1,710
2. 28 × 57 = 1,596
3. 47 × 63 = 2,961
4. 36 × 82 = 2,952
5. 53 × 74 = 3,922
6. 63 × 28 = 1,764
7. 39 × 45 = 1,755
8. 84 × 53 = 4,452
9. 28 × 39 = 1,092
10. 65 × 83 = 5,395
11. 48 × 63 = 3,024
12. 67 × 25 = 1,675
13. 27 × 49 = 1,323
14. 82 × 36 = 2,952
15. 24 × 93 = 2,232
16. 48 × 30 = 1,440
17. 83 × 62 = 5,146
18. 46 × 81 = 3,726
19. 57 × 38 = 2,166
20. 62 × 54 = 3,348
21. 76 × 46 = 3,496
22. 49 × 73 = 3,577
23. 54 × 18 = 972
24. 74 × 36 = 2,664
25. 68 × 24 = 1,632
26. 39 × 56 = 2,184
27. 63 × 42 = 2,646
28. 32 × 84 = 2,688
29. 65 × 45 = 2,925
30. 27 × 34 = 918

Anything's possible with practice!

Multiplication

Skill: Multiplying by Two-Digit Numbers

Name _____

Show your work on another sheet.
Write your answers here.

Total Problems __30__

Problems Correct _____

1. 326 × 14 = 4,564
2. 345 × 23 = 7,935
3. 265 × 13 = 3,445
4. 416 × 25 = 10,400
5. 364 × 18 = 6,552
6. 516 × 32 = 16,512
7. 365 × 41 = 14,965
8. 423 × 51 = 21,573
9. 363 × 23 = 8,349
10. 245 × 34 = 8,330
11. 523 × 15 = 7,845
12. 142 × 28 = 3,976
13. 212 × 45 = 9,540
14. 234 × 36 = 8,424
15. 325 × 24 = 7,800
16. 232 × 19 = 4,408
17. 425 × 43 = 18,275
18. 443 × 24 = 10,632
19. 312 × 52 = 16,224
20. 286 × 34 = 9,724
21. 132 × 41 = 5,412
22. 284 × 26 = 7,384
23. 429 × 58 = 24,882
24. 235 × 28 = 6,580
25. 516 × 48 = 24,768
26. 425 × 38 = 16,150
27. 235 × 72 = 16,920
28. 142 × 63 = 8,946
29. 323 × 45 = 14,535
30. 261 × 34 = 8,874

Practice makes perfect!

Multiplication

Skill: Multiplication With Zeros

Name _____

Show your work on another sheet.
Write your answers here.

Total Problems __30__

Problems Correct _____

1. 407 × 39 = 15,873
2. 530 × 62 = 32,860
3. 261 × 40 = 10,440
4. 704 × 82 = 57,728
5. 607 × 53 = 32,171
6. 437 × 20 = 8,740
7. 623 × 30 = 18,690
8. 140 × 57 = 7,980
9. 210 × 78 = 16,380
10. 527 × 30 = 15,810
11. 708 × 23 = 16,284
12. 283 × 40 = 11,320
13. 340 × 68 = 23,120
14. 630 × 24 = 15,120
15. 208 × 40 = 8,320
16. 896 × 30 = 26,880
17. 730 × 52 = 37,960
18. 347 × 80 = 27,760
19. 310 × 64 = 19,840
20. 488 × 20 = 9,760
21. 107 × 46 = 4,922
22. 830 × 71 = 58,930
23. 748 × 50 = 37,400
24. 560 × 36 = 20,160
25. 205 × 94 = 19,270
26. 827 × 70 = 57,890
27. 736 × 20 = 14,720
28. 506 × 44 = 22,264
29. 830 × 64 = 53,120
30. 463 × 50 = 23,150

Practice hard. You'll win.

Multiplication

Skill: Multiplying by Two-Digit Numbers

Name _____

Show your work on another sheet.
Write your answers here.

Total Problems __30__

Problems Correct _____

1. 436 × 28 = 12,208
2. 327 × 51 = 16,677
3. 824 × 32 = 26,368
4. 528 × 63 = 33,264
5. 232 × 82 = 19,024
6. 329 × 18 = 5,922
7. 252 × 45 = 11,340
8. 362 × 54 = 19,548
9. 243 × 84 = 20,412
10. 392 × 41 = 16,072
11. 354 × 25 = 8,850
12. 236 × 57 = 13,452
13. 583 × 32 = 18,656
14. 442 × 23 = 10,166
15. 623 × 52 = 32,396
16. 542 × 78 = 42,276
17. 825 × 43 = 35,475
18. 514 × 62 = 31,868
19. 362 × 54 = 19,548
20. 424 × 49 = 20,776
21. 282 × 91 = 25,662
22. 989 × 22 = 21,758
23. 418 × 35 = 14,630
24. 683 × 83 = 56,689
25. 536 × 24 = 12,864
26. 817 × 53 = 43,301
27. 724 × 46 = 33,304
28. 325 × 72 = 23,400
29. 824 × 56 = 46,144
30. 633 × 38 = 24,054

Success ahoy! Just practice!

Math IF8740

Answer Key

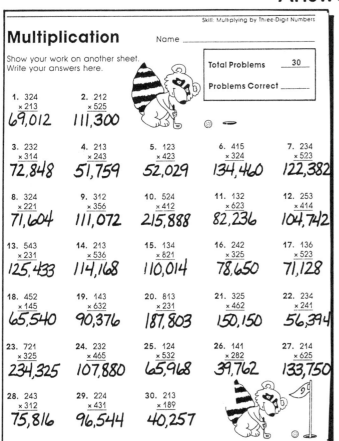

Multiplication

Name _____

Show your work on another sheet.
Write your answers here.

Total Problems _____30_____

Problems Correct _____

1. 324
    × 213
    69,012

2. 212
    × 525
    111,300

3. 232
    × 314
    72,848

4. 213
    × 243
    51,759

5. 123
    × 423
    52,029

6. 415
    × 324
    134,460

7. 234
    × 523
    122,382

8. 324
    × 221
    71,604

9. 312
    × 356
    111,072

10. 524
    × 412
    215,888

11. 132
    × 623
    82,236

12. 253
    × 414
    104,742

13. 543
    × 231
    125,433

14. 213
    × 536
    114,168

15. 134
    × 821
    110,014

16. 242
    × 325
    78,650

17. 136
    × 523
    71,128

18. 452
    × 145
    65,540

19. 143
    × 632
    90,376

20. 813
    × 231
    187,803

21. 325
    × 462
    150,150

22. 234
    × 241
    56,394

23. 721
    × 325
    234,325

24. 232
    × 465
    107,880

25. 124
    × 532
    65,968

26. 141
    × 282
    39,762

27. 214
    × 625
    133,750

28. 243
    × 312
    75,816

29. 224
    × 431
    96,544

30. 213
    × 189
    40,257

Division

Name _____

Total Problems _____31_____

Problems Correct _____

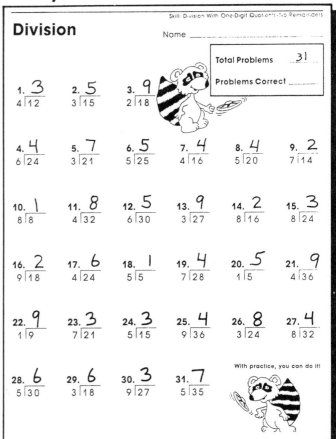

1. **3** 4)12
2. **5** 3)15
3. **9** 2)18
4. **4** 6)24
5. **7** 3)21
6. **5** 5)25
7. **4** 4)16
8. **4** 5)20
9. **2** 7)14
10. **1** 8)8
11. **8** 4)32
12. **5** 6)30
13. **9** 3)27
14. **2** 8)16
15. **3** 8)24
16. **2** 9)18
17. **6** 4)24
18. **1** 5)5
19. **4** 7)28
20. **5** 1)5
21. **9** 4)36
22. **9** 1)9
23. **3** 7)21
24. **3** 5)15
25. **4** 9)36
26. **8** 3)24
27. **4** 8)32
28. **6** 5)30
29. **6** 3)18
30. **3** 9)27
31. **7** 5)35

With practice, you can do it!

Division

Name _____

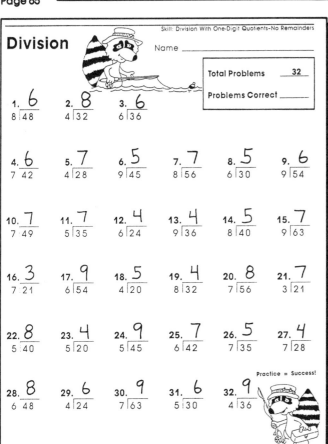

Total Problems _____32_____

Problems Correct _____

1. **6** 8)48
2. **8** 4)32
3. **6** 6)36
4. **6** 7)42
5. **7** 4)28
6. **5** 9)45
7. **7** 8)56
8. **5** 6)30
9. **6** 9)54
10. **7** 7)49
11. **7** 5)35
12. **4** 6)24
13. **4** 9)36
14. **5** 8)40
15. **7** 9)63
16. **3** 7)21
17. **9** 6)54
18. **5** 4)20
19. **4** 8)32
20. **8** 7)56
21. **7** 3)21
22. **8** 5)40
23. **4** 5)20
24. **9** 5)45
25. **7** 6)42
26. **5** 7)35
27. **4** 7)28
28. **8** 6)48
29. **6** 4)24
30. **9** 7)63
31. **6** 5)30
32. **9** 4)36

Practice = Success!

Division

Name _____

Total Problems _____32_____

Problems Correct _____

1. **8** 6)48
2. **4** 7)28
3. **6** 7)42
4. **7** 8)56
5. **4** 6)24
6. **7** 5)35
7. **8** 8)64
8. **5** 6)30
9. **7** 9)63
10. **7** 7)49
11. **5** 8)40
12. **6** 9)54
13. **8** 4)32
14. **9** 5)45
15. **8** 7)56
16. **9** 4)36
17. **6** 5)30
18. **9** 7)63
19. **9** 8)72
20. **5** 7)35
21. **8** 5)40
22. **9** 9)81
23. **7** 4)28
24. **6** 4)24
25. **9** 6)54
26. **6** 6)36
27. **8** 9)72
28. **6** 8)48
29. **4** 9)36
30. **7** 6)42
31. **5** 9)45
32. **4** 8)32

Anything's possible with practice!

Answer Key

Division
Skill: Division With One-Digit Quotients-No Remainders

Name _____

Total Problems __32__
Problems Correct _____

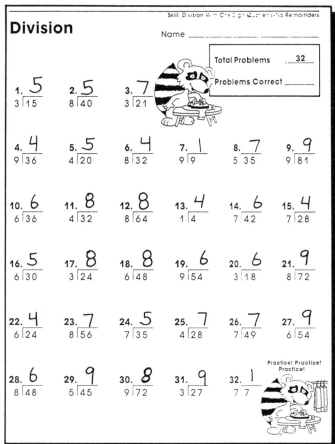

1. 5 — 3√15
2. 5 — 8√40
3. 7 — 3√21

4. 4 — 9√36
5. 5 — 4√20
6. 4 — 8√32
7. 1 — 9√9
8. 7 — 5√35
9. 9 — 9√81

10. 6 — 6√36
11. 8 — 4√32
12. 8 — 8√64
13. 4 — 1√4
14. 6 — 7√42
15. 4 — 7√28

16. 5 — 6√30
17. 8 — 3√24
18. 8 — 6√48
19. 6 — 9√54
20. 6 — 3√18
21. 9 — 8√72

22. 4 — 6√24
23. 7 — 8√56
24. 5 — 7√35
25. 7 — 4√28
26. 7 — 7√49
27. 9 — 6√54

28. 6 — 8√48
29. 9 — 5√45
30. 8 — 9√72
31. 9 — 3√27
32. 1 — 7√7

Practice! Practice! Practice!

Page 69

Division
Skill: Long Division Through 9—With No Remainders

Name _____

Total Problems __38__
Problems Correct _____

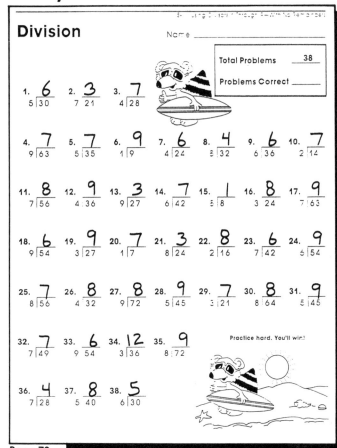

1. 6 — 5√30
2. 3 — 7√21
3. 7 — 4√28

4. 7 — 9√63
5. 7 — 5√35
6. 9 — 1√9
7. 6 — 4√24
8. 4 — 8√32
9. 6 — 6√36
10. 7 — 2√14

11. 8 — 7√56
12. 9 — 4√36
13. 3 — 9√27
14. 7 — 6√42
15. 1 — 8√8
16. 8 — 3√24
17. 9 — 7√63

18. 6 — 9√54
19. 9 — 3√27
20. 7 — 1√7
21. 3 — 8√24
22. 8 — 2√16
23. 6 — 7√42
24. 9 — 6√54

25. 7 — 8√56
26. 8 — 4√32
27. 8 — 9√72
28. 9 — 5√45
29. 7 — 3√21
30. 8 — 8√64
31. 9 — 5√45

32. 7 — 7√49
33. 6 — 9√54
34. 12 — 3√36
35. 9 — 8√72

Practice hard. You'll win!

36. 4 — 7√28
37. 8 — 5√40
38. 5 — 6√30

Page 70

Division
Skill: Division With One-Digit Quotients-Remainders

Name _____

Total Problems __30__
Problems Correct _____

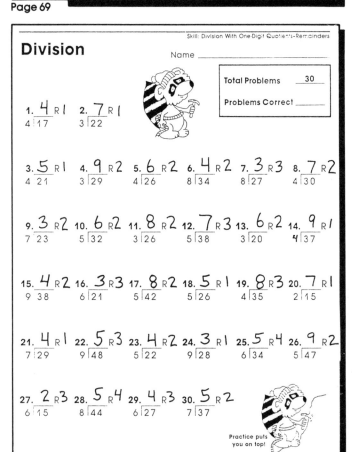

1. 4 R1 — 4√17
2. 7 R1 — 3√22

3. 5 R1 — 4√21
4. 9 R2 — 3√29
5. 6 R2 — 4√26
6. 4 R2 — 8√34
7. 3 R3 — 8√27
8. 7 R2 — 4√30

9. 3 R2 — 7√23
10. 6 R2 — 5√32
11. 8 R2 — 3√26
12. 7 R3 — 5√38
13. 6 R2 — 3√20
14. 9 R1 — 4√37

15. 4 R2 — 9√38
16. 3 R3 — 6√21
17. 8 R2 — 5√42
18. 5 R1 — 5√26
19. 8 R3 — 4√35
20. 7 R1 — 2√15

21. 4 R1 — 7√29
22. 5 R3 — 9√48
23. 4 R2 — 5√22
24. 3 R1 — 9√28
25. 5 R4 — 6√34
26. 9 R2 — 5√47

27. 2 R3 — 6√15
28. 5 R4 — 8√44
29. 4 R3 — 6√27
30. 5 R2 — 7√37

Practice puts you on top!

Page 71

Division
Skill: Division With One-Digit Quotients-Remainders

Name _____

Total Problems __30__
Problems Correct _____

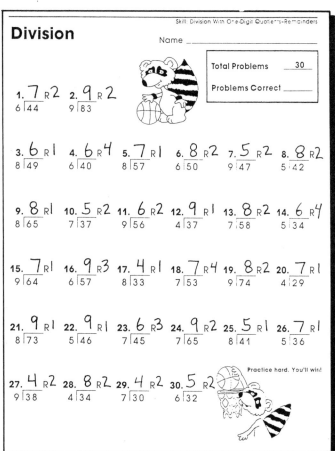

1. 7 R2 — 6√44
2. 9 R2 — 9√83

3. 6 R1 — 8√49
4. 6 R4 — 9√40
5. 7 R1 — 8√57
6. 8 R2 — 6√50
7. 5 R2 — 9√47
8. 8 R2 — 5√42

9. 8 R1 — 8√65
10. 5 R2 — 7√37
11. 6 R2 — 9√56
12. 9 R1 — 4√37
13. 8 R2 — 7√58
14. 6 R4 — 5√34

15. 7 R1 — 9√64
16. 9 R3 — 6√57
17. 4 R1 — 8√33
18. 7 R4 — 7√53
19. 8 R2 — 9√74
20. 7 R1 — 4√29

21. 9 R1 — 8√73
22. 9 R1 — 5√46
23. 6 R3 — 7√45
24. 9 R2 — 7√65
25. 5 R1 — 8√41
26. 7 R1 — 5√36

27. 4 R2 — 9√38
28. 8 R2 — 4√34
29. 4 R2 — 7√30
30. 5 R2 — 6√32

Practice hard. You'll win!

Page 72

Answer Key

Page 73

Division

Name _____

Total Problems   30

Problems Correct _____

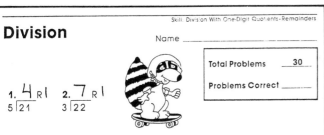

1. 4 R1
   5⟌21

2. 7 R1
   3⟌22

3. 6 R1
   3⟌19

4. 4 R2
   4⟌18

5. 5 R2
   5⟌27

6. 5 R1
   8⟌41

7. 8 R2
   4⟌34

8. 7 R2
   7⟌51

9. 6 R1
   7⟌43

10. 8 R1
    8⟌65

11. 3 R1
    6⟌19

12. 8 R2
    3⟌26

13. 9 R1
    2⟌19

14. 7 R1
    8⟌57

15. 8 R1
    6⟌49

16. 8 R1
    2⟌17

17. 9 R2
    3⟌29

18. 6 R2
    5⟌32

19. 9 R2
    9⟌83

20. 7 R2
    6⟌44

21. 9 R2
    5⟌47

22. 6 R2
    6⟌38

23. 6 R1
    2⟌13

24. 3 R1
    5⟌16

25. 6 R2
    3⟌20

26. 7 R1
    9⟌64

27. 6 R3
    8⟌51

28. 9 R1
    8⟌73

29. 8 R3
    5⟌43

30. 9 R5
    7⟌68

With practice, you can do it!

Page 73

Page 74

Division

Show your work on another sheet
Write your answers here.

Name _____

Total Problems   32

Problems Correct _____

1. 4 R2
   7⟌30

2. 5 R3
   8⟌43

3. 8 R3
   9⟌75

4. 4 R2
   6⟌26

5. 5 R2
   5⟌27

6. 3 R2
   8⟌26

7. 8 R4
   6⟌52

8. 4 R3
   9⟌39

9. 8 R2
   4⟌34

10. 5 R3
    9⟌48

11. 5 R3
    7⟌38

12. 7 R1
    3⟌22

13. 7 R2
    5⟌37

14. 6 R2
    6⟌38

15. 5 R3
    6⟌33

16. 8 R2
    3⟌26

17. 7 R2
    8⟌58

18. 7 R2
    7⟌51

19. 9 R3
    9⟌84

20. 7 R2
    4⟌30

21. 5 R2
    4⟌22

22. 7 R1
    9⟌64

23. 7 R3
    6⟌45

24. 8 R2
    8⟌66

25. 9 R2
    7⟌65

26. 9 R1
    2⟌19

27. 8 R1
    2⟌17

28. 4 R2
    8⟌34

29. 5 R3
    5⟌28

Practice makes perfect!

30. 6 R3
    9⟌57

31. 3 R3
    7⟌24

32. 9 R2
    3⟌29

Page 74

Page 75

Division

Show your work on another sheet.
Write your answers here.

Name _____

Total Problems   32

Problems Correct _____

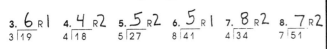

1. 9 R2
   8⟌74

2. 6 R2
   5⟌32

3. 8 R2
   6⟌50

4. 6 R2
   3⟌20

5. 5 R5
   9⟌50

6. 8 R3
   7⟌59

7. 9 R2
   4⟌38

8. 6 R2
   8⟌50

9. 6 R3
   4⟌27

10. 5 R2
    9⟌47

11. 7 R5
    8⟌61

12. 5 R5
    7⟌40

13. 9 R3
    6⟌57

14. 9 R1
    9⟌82

15. 5 R1
    2⟌11

16. 6 R6
    7⟌48

17. 8 R1
    9⟌73

18. 9 R2
    5⟌47

19. 7 R2
    6⟌44

20. 9 R5
    7⟌68

21. 5 R2
    3⟌17

22. 5 R7
    8⟌47

23. 5 R1
    3⟌31

24. 8 R3
    5⟌43

25. 9 R6
    9⟌87

26. 9 R1
    3⟌28

27. 3 R2
    6⟌20

28. 4 R2
    9⟌38

29. 6 R1
    2⟌13

Practice! Practice! Practice!

30. 3 R6
    7⟌27

31. 4 R7
    8⟌39

32. 8 R3
    4⟌35

Page 75

Page 76

Division

Show your work on another sheet.
Write your answers here.

Name _____

Total Problems   32

Problems Correct _____

1. 23
   2⟌46

2. 31
   3⟌93

3. 21
   4⟌84

4. 10
   9⟌90

5. 34
   2⟌68

6. 11
   7⟌77

7. 12
   4⟌48

8. 21
   3⟌63

9. 11
   8⟌88

10. 12
    2⟌24

11. 12
    3⟌36

12. 10
    5⟌50

13. 10
    6⟌60

14. 32
    2⟌64

15. 11
    4⟌44

16. 14
    2⟌28

17. 33
    3⟌99

18. 33
    2⟌66

19. 31
    2⟌62

20. 23
    3⟌69

21. 41
    2⟌82

22. 11
    6⟌66

23. 24
    2⟌48

24. 13
    3⟌39

25. 11
    9⟌99

26. 42
    2⟌84

27. 11
    5⟌55

28. 10
    8⟌80

29. 43
    2⟌86

With practice, you can do it!

30. 13
    2⟌26

31. 10
    7⟌70

32. 32
    3⟌96

Page 76

Answer Key

Page 77

Division

Skill: Division With Two-Digit Quotients (With Remainders)

Name _____

Show your work on another sheet.
Write your answers here.

Total Problems ___32___

Problems Correct _____

1. 22R2 3)68
2. 28R2 3)86

3. 23R1 2)47
4. 11R2 5)57
5. 11R1 8)89
6. 31R2 3)95
7. 11R2 7)79
8. 32R1 2)65

9. 21R3 4)87
10. 12R1 3)37
11. 11R4 5)59
12. 43R1 2)87
13. 11R1 4)45
14. 21R1 3)64

15. 4R1 2)83
16. 12R1 8)97
17. 13R1 6)79
18. 16R1 4)65
19. 13R4 7)95
20. 24R2 3)74

21. 14R2 5)72
22. 26R1 2)53
23. 12R2 7)86
24. 15R2 3)47
25. 13R3 6)81
26. 13R1 4)53

27. 12R2 8)98
28. 18R1 3)55
29. 12R3 6)75

Success ahoy! Just practice!

30. 17R3 4)71
31. 17R1 2)35
32. 18R3 5)93

Page 77

Page 78

Division

Skill: Division With Two-Digit Quotients (With Remainders)

Name _____

Show your work on another sheet.
Write your answers here.

Total Problems ___32___

Problems Correct _____

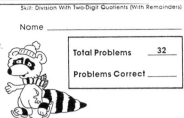

1. 15R2 6)92
2. 15R3 4)63

3. 18R1 2)37
4. 13R5 7)96
5. 18R2 3)56
6. 12R3 5)63
7. 12R3 8)99
8. 13R3 4)55

9. 14R1 6)85
10. 14R4 5)74
11. 37R1 2)75
12. 23R3 4)95
13. 11R5 7)82
14. 28R1 3)85

15. 11R7 8)95
16. 18R3 4)75
17. 16R2 5)82
18. 25R2 3)77
19. 14R5 6)89
20. 28R1 2)57

21. 13R2 7)93
22. 14R4 5)74
23. 46R1 2)93
24. 16R3 4)67
25. 14R1 3)43
26. 15R5 6)95

27. 38R1 2)77
28. 11R5 8)93
29. 19R1 3)58

30. 18R4 5)94
31. 12R1 7)85
32. 11R5 6)71

Practice = Success!

Page 78

Page 79

Division

Skill: Division With Two-Digit Quotients (With No Remainders)

Name _____

Show your work on another sheet.
Write your answers here.

Total Problems ___27___

Problems Correct _____

1. 75 3)225
2. 54 6)324

3. 32 9)288
4. 69 2)138
5. 65 7)455
6. 54 4)216
7. 63 8)504

8. 54 5)270
9. 57 3)171
10. 63 6)378
11. 95 9)855
12. 97 2)194

13. 55 7)385
14. 76 4)304
15. 87 5)435
16. 67 3)201
17. 58 6)348

18. 93 8)744
19. 77 2)154
20. 34 9)306
21. 56 4)224
22. 92 7)644

23. 95 5)475
24. 94 3)282
25. 98 6)588

Practice hard. You'll win!

26. 28 9)252
27. 88 2)176

Page 79

Page 80

Division

Skill: Division With Two-Digit Quotients (With Remainders)

Name _____

Show your work on another sheet.
Write your answers here.

Total Problems ___32___

Problems Correct _____

1. 77R1 2)155
2. 89R2 4)358

3. 45R3 6)273
4. 53R4 8)428
5. 44R3 9)399
6. 98R2 3)296
7. 58R1 5)291
8. 78R3 7)549

9. 86R1 2)173
10. 87R4 5)439
11. 84R2 9)758
12. 65R2 6)392
13. 39R6 7)279
14. 69R2 3)209

15. 57R3 4)231
16. 87R3 8)699
17. 59R1 2)119
18. 84R3 6)507
19. 39R2 5)197
20. 54R3 9)479

21. 57R2 3)173
22. 52R4 7)408
23. 39R3 6)237
24. 67R3 5)338
25. 78R2 4)314
26. 48R5 8)389

27. 27R2 9)245
28. 47R3 5)238
29. 68R1 2)137

30. 98R1 3)295
31. 74R5 8)597
32. 53R1 6)319

Page 80

Answer Key

Page 81

Division

Skill: Division With Two-Digit Quotients (With Remainders)

Name _____

Show your work on another sheet.
Write your answers here.

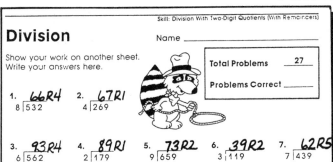

Total Problems ___27___

Problems Correct _____

1. 66R4
8|532

2. 67R1
4|269

3. 93R4
6|562

4. 89R1
2|179

5. 73R2
9|659

6. 39R2
3|119

7. 62R5
7|439

8. 96R4
5|484

9. 38R3
4|155

10. 65R2
9|587

11. 94R5
8|757

12. 78R1
2|157

13. 47R2
3|143

14. 56R2
6|338

15. 96R1
2|193

16. 47R2
7|331

17. 32R3
9|291

18. 26R2
8|210

19. 95R3
4|383

20. 74R2
3|224

21. 74R4
5|374

22. 89R3
6|537

23. 96R3
9|867

24. 67R1
2|135

25. 74R2
6|446

Practice! Practice! Practice!

26. 84R2
3|254

27. 38R3
8|307

Page 81

Page 82

Division

Skill: Division With Three-Digit Quotients (With No Remainders)

Name _____

Show your work on another sheet.
Write your answers here.

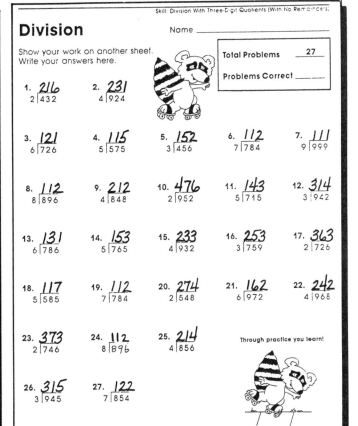

Total Problems ___27___

Problems Correct _____

1. 216
2|432

2. 231
4|924

3. 121
6|726

4. 115
5|575

5. 152
3|456

6. 112
7|784

7. 111
9|999

8. 112
8|896

9. 212
4|848

10. 476
2|952

11. 143
5|715

12. 314
3|942

13. 131
6|786

14. 153
5|765

15. 233
4|932

16. 253
3|759

17. 363
2|726

18. 117
5|585

19. 112
7|784

20. 274
2|548

21. 162
6|972

22. 242
4|968

23. 373
2|746

24. 112
8|896

25. 214
4|856

Through practice you learn!

26. 315
3|945

27. 122
7|854

Page 82

Page 83

Division

Skill: Division With Three-Digit Quotients (With Remainders)

Name _____

Show your work on another sheet.
Write your answers here.

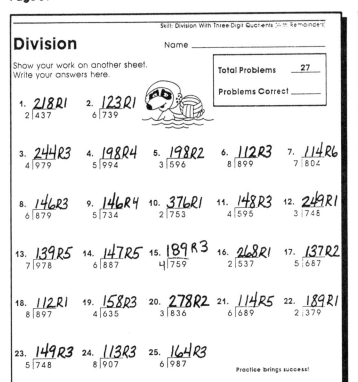

Total Problems ___27___

Problems Correct _____

1. 218R1
2|437

2. 123R1
6|739

3. 244R3
4|979

4. 198R4
5|994

5. 198R2
3|596

6. 112R3
8|899

7. 114R6
7|804

8. 146R3
6|879

9. 146R4
5|734

10. 376R1
2|753

11. 148R3
4|595

12. 249R1
3|748

13. 139R5
7|978

14. 147R5
6|887

15. 189R3
4|759

16. 268R1
2|537

17. 137R2
5|687

18. 112R1
8|897

19. 158R3
4|635

20. 278R2
3|836

21. 114R5
6|689

22. 189R1
2|379

23. 149R3
5|748

24. 113R3
8|907

25. 164R3
6|987

Practice brings success!

26. 122R4
7|858

27. 168R3
4|675

Page 83

Page 84

Division

Skill: Division With Three-Digit Quotients (With Remainders)

Name _____

Show your work on another sheet.
Write your answers here.

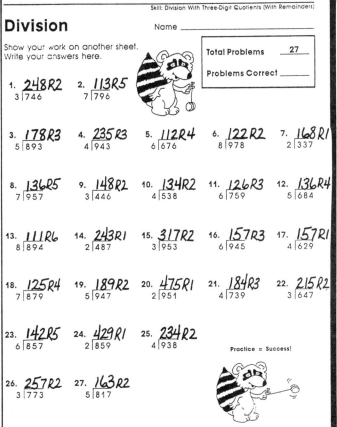

Total Problems ___27___

Problems Correct _____

1. 248R2
3|746

2. 113R5
7|796

3. 178R3
5|893

4. 235R3
4|943

5. 112R4
6|676

6. 122R2
8|978

7. 168R1
2|337

8. 136R5
7|957

9. 148R2
3|446

10. 134R2
4|538

11. 126R3
6|759

12. 136R4
5|684

13. 111R6
8|894

14. 243R1
2|487

15. 317R2
3|953

16. 157R3
6|945

17. 157R1
4|629

18. 125R4
7|879

19. 189R2
5|947

20. 475R1
2|951

21. 184R3
4|739

22. 215R2
3|647

23. 142R5
6|857

24. 429R1
2|859

25. 234R2
4|938

Practice = Success!

26. 257R2
3|773

27. 163R2
5|817

Page 84

Answer Key

Page 85

Division

Skill: Dividing With Zero in the Quotient

Name _____

Show your work on another sheet.
Write your answers here.

Total Problems ___27___

Problems Correct _____

1. $10R5$ — $6\overline{)65}$ 2. $10R4$ — $9\overline{)94}$

3. $308R1$ — $3\overline{)925}$ 4. $80R4$ — $7\overline{)564}$ 5. $205R3$ — $4\overline{)823}$ 6. $50R3$ — $5\overline{)253}$ 7. $108R1$ — $8\overline{)865}$

8. $420R1$ — $2\overline{)841}$ 9. $10R5$ — $7\overline{)75}$ 10. $60R4$ — $6\overline{)364}$ 11. $103R2$ — $4\overline{)414}$ 12. $80R4$ — $5\overline{)404}$

13. $40R7$ — $8\overline{)327}$ 14. $207R2$ — $3\overline{)623}$ 15. $230R1$ — $2\overline{)461}$ 16. $60R3$ — $7\overline{)423}$ 17. $104R3$ — $6\overline{)627}$

18. $105R4$ — $5\overline{)529}$ 19. $210R2$ — $4\overline{)842}$ 20. $320R1$ — $3\overline{)961}$ 21. $40R5$ — $8\overline{)325}$ 22. $105R3$ — $7\overline{)738}$

23. $70R3$ — $6\overline{)423}$ 24. $120R1$ — $2\overline{)241}$ 25. $107R4$ — $5\overline{)539}$

Success ahoy! Just practice!

26. $90R2$ — $3\overline{)272}$ 27. $20R3$ — $4\overline{)83}$

Page 86

Division

Skill: Dividing With Zero in the Quotient

Name _____

Show your work on another sheet.
Write your answers here.

Total Problems ___27___

Problems Correct _____

1. $10R7$ — $8\overline{)87}$ 2. $10R3$ — $5\overline{)53}$

3. $210R2$ — $4\overline{)842}$ 4. $60R6$ — $7\overline{)426}$ 5. $30R2$ — $3\overline{)92}$ 6. $80R4$ — $6\overline{)484}$ 7. $104R7$ — $8\overline{)839}$

8. $307R1$ — $2\overline{)615}$ 9. $10R8$ — $9\overline{)98}$ 10. $90R3$ — $6\overline{)543}$ 11. $10R3$ — $7\overline{)73}$ 12. $120R3$ — $4\overline{)483}$

13. $90R2$ — $3\overline{)272}$ 14. $103R2$ — $5\overline{)517}$ 15. $90R4$ — $7\overline{)634}$ 16. $407R1$ — $2\overline{)815}$ 17. $60R4$ — $6\overline{)364}$

18. $80R3$ — $4\overline{)323}$ 19. $90R6$ — $8\overline{)726}$ 20. $210R1$ — $3\overline{)631}$ 21. $105R2$ — $6\overline{)632}$ 22. $90R3$ — $5\overline{)453}$

23. $105R3$ — $7\overline{)738}$ 24. $210R1$ — $2\overline{)421}$ 25. $104R2$ — $9\overline{)938}$

Practice brings success!

26. $105R1$ — $5\overline{)526}$ 27. $70R3$ — $4\overline{)283}$

Page 87

Division

Skill: Division With Three- and Four-Digit Quotients (With and Without Remainders)

Name _____

Snow your work on another sheet.
Write your answers here.

Total Problems ___27___

Problems Correct _____

1. $1,743$ — $2\overline{)3,486}$ 2. $2,143$ — $4\overline{)8,572}$

3. $627R2$ — $6\overline{)3,764}$ 4. $1,065R3$ — $5\overline{)5,328}$ 5. 958 — $3\overline{)2,874}$ 6. $4,248R1$ — $2\overline{)8,497}$ 7. $1,228R2$ — $7\overline{)8,598}$

8. $4,020$ — $2\overline{)8,040}$ 9. 747 — $4\overline{)2,988}$ 10. $1,358R1$ — $6\overline{)8,149}$ 11. $714R3$ — $7\overline{)5,001}$ 12. $2,079R1$ — $3\overline{)6,238}$

13. $1,476R4$ — $5\overline{)7,384}$ 14. 547 — $8\overline{)4,376}$ 15. $2,405R1$ — $2\overline{)4,811}$ 16. $395R3$ — $4\overline{)1,583}$ 17. $1,231R5$ — $6\overline{)7,391}$

18. $2,314R1$ — $3\overline{)6,943}$ 19. 685 — $7\overline{)4,795}$ 20. $1,047R2$ — $5\overline{)5,237}$ 21. $585R7$ — $8\overline{)4,687}$ 22. $3,420R1$ — $2\overline{)6,841}$

23. $2,258R3$ — $4\overline{)9,035}$ 24. $1,578R1$ — $6\overline{)9,469}$ 25. $2,079R1$ — $3\overline{)6,238}$

Practice hard. You'll win!

26. $313R2$ — $9\overline{)2,819}$ 27. $676R1$ — $5\overline{)3,381}$

Page 88

Division

Skill: Division With Two-Digit Divisors (With Remainders)

Name _____

Show your work on another sheet.
Write your answers here.

Total Problems ___27___

Problems Correct _____

1. $3R1$ — $21\overline{)64}$ 2. $2R9$ — $42\overline{)93}$

3. $2R6$ — $34\overline{)74}$ 4. $6R3$ — $12\overline{)75}$ 5. $2R6$ — $45\overline{)96}$ 6. $3R10$ — $24\overline{)82}$ 7. $2R12$ — $37\overline{)86}$

8. $5R3$ — $14\overline{)73}$ 9. $2R1$ — $48\overline{)97}$ 10. $4R5$ — $16\overline{)69}$ 11. $3R6$ — $29\overline{)93}$ 12. $2R7$ — $40\overline{)87}$

13. $3R7$ — $18\overline{)61}$ 14. $2R7$ — $38\overline{)83}$ 15. $3R1$ — $27\overline{)82}$ 16. $1R18$ — $76\overline{)94}$ 17. $4R12$ — $19\overline{)88}$

18. $6R1$ — $14\overline{)85}$ 19. $3R12$ — $28\overline{)96}$ 20. $4R5$ — $17\overline{)73}$ 21. $2R11$ — $25\overline{)61}$ 22. $3R1$ — $23\overline{)70}$

23. $5R9$ — $15\overline{)84}$ 24. $4R2$ — $22\overline{)90}$ 25. $2R11$ — $35\overline{)81}$

Through practice you learn!

26. $7R5$ — $13\overline{)96}$ 27. $5R3$ — $18\overline{)93}$

Answer Key

Page 89

Skill: Division With Two-Digit Divisors (With Remainders)

Division

Name _____

Show your work on another sheet.
Write your answers here.

Total Problems ___27___

Problems Correct _____

1. 6R10 34⟌214
2. 9R2 63⟌569

3. 6R4 81⟌490
4. 7R11 23⟌172
5. 8R11 15⟌131
6. 5R7 37⟌192
7. 8R13 24⟌205

8. 6R7 78⟌475
9. 5R13 92⟌473
10. 8R14 46⟌382
11. 6R30 67⟌432
12. 7R6 21⟌153

13. 8R14 32⟌270
14. 9R29 86⟌803
15. 6R12 74⟌456
16. 8R13 31⟌261
17. 6R31 65⟌421

18. 7R19 41⟌306
19. 9R29 68⟌641
20. 8R16 38⟌320
21. 9R10 28⟌262
22. 6R27 49⟌321

23. 8R33 79⟌665
24. 6R9 27⟌171
25. 7R16 83⟌597

26. 9R21 34⟌327
27. 5R22 58⟌312

Page 89

Page 90

Skill: Division With Two-Digit Divisors (With Remainders)

Division

Name _____

Show your work on another sheet.
Write your answers here.

Total Problems ___27___

Problems Correct _____

1. 9R6 14⟌132
2. 8R12 23⟌196

3. 9R12 64⟌588
4. 7R23 83⟌604
5. 8R35 76⟌643
6. 6R22 92⟌574
7. 6R8 17⟌110

8. 8R6 26⟌214
9. 5R9 37⟌194
10. 9R4 53⟌481
11. 6R15 47⟌297
12. 7R9 25⟌184

13. 6R13 73⟌451
14. 9R38 87⟌821
15. 8R15 24⟌207
16. 6R13 34⟌217
17. 4R17 67⟌285

18. 6R13 68⟌421
19. 9R19 71⟌658
20. 8R12 32⟌268
21. 7R4 29⟌207
22. 9R44 57⟌557

23. 7R13 35⟌258
24. 8R25 27⟌241
25. 6R58 62⟌430

Anything's possible with practice!

26. 7R17 52⟌381
27. 9R24 38⟌366

Page 90

Page 91

Skill: Division With Two-Digit Divisors (With Remainders)

Division

Name _____

Show your work on another sheet.
Write your answers here.

Total Problems ___27___

Problems Correct _____

1. 14R11 26⟌375
2. 21R9 17⟌366

3. 17R23 47⟌822
4. 11R3 84⟌927
5. 64R9 12⟌777
6. 25R15 36⟌915
7. 15R32 58⟌902

8. 10R42 91⟌952
9. 17R47 53⟌948
10. 26R15 32⟌847
11. 14R3 71⟌997
12. 12R52 68⟌868

13. 11R63 75⟌888
14. 21R25 41⟌886
15. 10R13 82⟌833
16. 45R12 18⟌822
17. 26R21 31⟌827

18. 40R17 19⟌777
19. 23R14 35⟌819
20. 17R39 46⟌821
21. 10R37 94⟌977
22. 12R46 77⟌970

23. 11R27 88⟌995
24. 25R21 38⟌971
25. 13R46 57⟌787

Practice and anything's possible!

26. 19R27 43⟌844
27. 14R35 67⟌973

Page 91

Page 92

Skill: Division With Two-Digit Divisors (With Remainders)

Division

Name _____

Show your work on another sheet.
Write your answers here.

Total Problems ___27___

Problems Correct _____

1. 58R12 17⟌998
2. 15R19 23⟌364

3. 12R39 49⟌627
4. 26R14 36⟌950
5. 11R62 72⟌854
6. 36R13 26⟌949
7. 62R6 14⟌874

8. 23R15 32⟌751
9. 14R23 56⟌807
10. 68R11 13⟌895
11. 25R13 29⟌738
12. 12R36 46⟌588

13. 21R23 24⟌527
14. 16R38 42⟌710
15. 11R65 73⟌868
16. 20R9 39⟌789
17. 31R8 27⟌845

18. 50R14 15⟌764
19. 24R3 34⟌819
20. 23R16 25⟌591
21. 45R12 18⟌822
22. 12R6 53⟌642

23. 60R5 12⟌725
24. 17R21 38⟌667
25. 10R45 51⟌555

Practice hard. You'll win!

26. 31R3 29⟌902
27. 40R4 19⟌774

Page 92

Answer Key

Division

Name _____

Show your work on another sheet.
Write your answers here.

Total Problems _____ 25

Problems Correct _____

1. 21)4,284 = 204
2. 40)8,040 = 201
3. 15)3,045 = 203
4. 25)5,025 = 201
5. 12)6,024 = 502
6. 13)2,743 = 211
7. 41)4,551 = 111
8. 17)1,904 = 112
9. 22)4,642 = 211
10. 31)9,641 = 311
11. 52)5,252 = 101
12. 10)3,370 = 337
13. 40)8,440 = 211
14. 11)6,853 = 623
15. 21)6,594 = 314
16. 32)9,984 = 312
17. 45)9,045 = 201
18. 10)4,680 = 468
19. 12)6,372 = 531
20. 35)7,735 = 221
21. 24)5,088 = 212
22. 14)1,428 = 102
23. 61)6,771 = 111
24. 20)8,840 = 442
25. 32)6,752 = 211

Through practice you learn!

Page 93

Fractions

Name _____

Total Problems _____ 28

Problems Correct _____

1. $\frac{2}{6} + \frac{1}{6} = \frac{3}{6}$
2. $\frac{3}{7} + \frac{2}{7} = \frac{5}{7}$
3. $\frac{3}{4} + \frac{2}{4} = \frac{3}{4}$
4. $\frac{3}{9} + \frac{4}{9} = \frac{7}{9}$
5. $\frac{4}{8} + \frac{2}{8} = \frac{6}{8}$
6. $\frac{1}{5} + \frac{3}{5} = \frac{4}{5}$
7. $\frac{3}{10} + \frac{6}{10} = \frac{9}{10}$
8. $\frac{4}{12} + \frac{6}{12} = \frac{10}{12}$
9. $\frac{2}{5} + \frac{3}{5} = \frac{5}{5}$
10. $\frac{4}{9} + \frac{4}{9} = \frac{8}{9}$
11. $\frac{5}{10} + \frac{2}{10} = \frac{7}{10}$
12. $\frac{4}{7} + \frac{1}{7} = \frac{5}{7}$
13. $\frac{1}{2} + \frac{1}{2} = \frac{2}{2}$
14. $\frac{3}{8} + \frac{2}{8} = \frac{7}{8}$
15. $\frac{3}{6} + \frac{1}{6} = \frac{4}{6}$
16. $\frac{6}{7} + \frac{1}{7} = \frac{7}{7}$
17. $\frac{4}{8} + \frac{4}{8} = \frac{8}{8}$
18. $\frac{2}{6} + \frac{2}{6} = \frac{4}{6}$
19. $\frac{1}{3} + \frac{2}{3} = \frac{3}{3}$
20. $\frac{2}{5} + \frac{2}{5} = \frac{4}{5}$
21. $\frac{5}{12} + \frac{3}{12} = \frac{8}{12}$
22. $\frac{5}{9} + \frac{3}{9} = \frac{8}{9}$
23. $\frac{2}{4} + \frac{2}{4} = \frac{4}{4}$
24. $\frac{7}{12} + \frac{3}{12} = \frac{10}{12}$
25. $\frac{1}{5} + \frac{4}{5} = \frac{5}{5}$
26. $\frac{2}{7} + \frac{4}{7} = \frac{6}{7}$
27. $\frac{3}{8} + \frac{4}{8} = \frac{7}{8}$
28. $\frac{2}{10} + \frac{3}{10} = \frac{5}{10}$

Practice! Practice! Practice!

Page 94

Fractions

Name _____

Total Problems _____ 28

Problems Correct _____

1. $\frac{3}{6} - \frac{1}{6} = \frac{2}{6}$
2. $\frac{7}{8} - \frac{5}{8} = \frac{2}{8}$
3. $\frac{7}{10} - \frac{4}{10} = \frac{3}{10}$
4. $\frac{4}{4} - \frac{3}{4} = \frac{1}{4}$
5. $\frac{8}{9} - \frac{4}{9} = \frac{4}{9}$
6. $\frac{11}{12} - \frac{5}{12} = \frac{6}{12}$
7. $\frac{7}{9} - \frac{5}{9} = \frac{2}{9}$
8. $\frac{4}{5} - \frac{2}{5} = \frac{2}{5}$
9. $\frac{6}{7} - \frac{4}{7} = \frac{2}{7}$
10. $\frac{3}{5} - \frac{2}{5} = \frac{1}{5}$
11. $\frac{8}{8} - \frac{5}{8} = \frac{3}{8}$
12. $\frac{9}{9} - \frac{2}{9} = \frac{7}{9}$
13. $\frac{Y}{10} - \frac{7}{10} = \frac{2}{10}$
14. $\frac{4}{2} - \frac{1}{2} = \frac{1}{2}$
15. $\frac{5}{6} - \frac{4}{6} = \frac{1}{6}$
16. $\frac{11}{12} - \frac{8}{12} = \frac{3}{12}$
17. $\frac{6}{6} - \frac{2}{6} = \frac{4}{6}$
18. $\frac{7}{8} - \frac{7}{8} = 0$
19. $\frac{3}{4} - \frac{1}{4} = \frac{2}{4}$
20. $\frac{7}{7} - \frac{4}{7} = \frac{3}{7}$
21. $\frac{10}{12} - \frac{6}{12} = \frac{4}{12}$
22. $\frac{1}{2} - \frac{1}{2} = 0$
23. $\frac{5}{5} - \frac{1}{5} = \frac{4}{5}$
24. $\frac{12}{12} - \frac{8}{12} = \frac{4}{12}$
25. $\frac{5}{9} - \frac{3}{9} = \frac{2}{9}$
26. $\frac{6}{10} - \frac{4}{10} = \frac{2}{10}$
27. $\frac{6}{6} - \frac{3}{6} = \frac{3}{6}$
28. $\frac{4}{7} - \frac{1}{7} = \frac{3}{7}$

Anything's possible with practice!

Page 95

Mixed Numerals

Name _____

Total Problems _____ 25

Problems Correct _____

1. $3\frac{2}{5} + 5\frac{1}{5} = 8\frac{3}{5}$
2. $4\frac{1}{6} + 5\frac{4}{6} = 9\frac{5}{6}$
3. $8\frac{1}{4} + 3\frac{2}{4} = 11\frac{3}{4}$
4. $3\frac{1}{5} + 9\frac{1}{5} = 12\frac{2}{5}$
5. $6\frac{3}{7} + 2\frac{2}{7} = 8\frac{5}{7}$
6. $8\frac{1}{9} + 3\frac{6}{9} = 11\frac{7}{9}$
7. $7\frac{2}{12} + 9\frac{3}{12} = 16\frac{5}{12}$
8. $5\frac{1}{3} + 7\frac{1}{3} = 12\frac{2}{3}$
9. $6\frac{1}{8} + 5\frac{2}{8} = 11\frac{3}{8}$
10. $4\frac{3}{7} + 9\frac{3}{7} = 13\frac{6}{7}$
11. $9\frac{1}{4} + 8\frac{2}{4} = 17\frac{3}{4}$
12. $7\frac{2}{5} + 3\frac{1}{5} = 10\frac{3}{5}$
13. $9\frac{3}{6} + 2\frac{1}{6} = 11\frac{4}{6}$
14. $4\frac{1}{2} + 6\frac{1}{2} = 10\frac{7}{2}$
15. $6\frac{4}{10} + 7\frac{5}{10} = 13\frac{9}{10}$
16. $6\frac{3}{8} + 9\frac{4}{8} = 15\frac{7}{8}$
17. $9\frac{5}{12} + 7\frac{6}{12} = 16\frac{4}{12}$
18. $7\frac{2}{8} + 7\frac{5}{8} = 14\frac{7}{8}$
19. $6\frac{5}{7} + 9\frac{1}{7} = 15\frac{6}{7}$
20. $9\frac{4}{7} + 8\frac{1}{7} = 17\frac{5}{7}$
21. $3\frac{1}{4} + 1\frac{1}{4} = 4\frac{3}{4}$
22. $8\frac{3}{10} + 5\frac{6}{10} = 13\frac{9}{10}$
23. $5\frac{1}{6} + 9\frac{3}{6} = 14\frac{5}{6}$
24. $7\frac{4}{12} + 8\frac{4}{12} = 15\frac{9}{12}$
25. $4\frac{3}{9} + 7\frac{4}{9} = 11\frac{7}{9}$

Practice = Success!

Page 96